HISTORY AND ILLUSION IN POI

The distinguished political philosopher Raymond Geuss examines critically some of the most widely held and important preconceptions about contemporary politics held in advanced Western societies. In a series of analytically focused chapters Dr Geuss discusses the state, authority, violence and coercion, the concept of legitimacy, liberalism, toleration, freedom, democracy, and human rights. He argues that the liberal democratic state committed to the defence of human rights is a historically contingent conjunction of disparate elements that do not fit together coherently. One of Geuss' most striking claims is that it makes sense to speak of rights only relative to a mechanism for enforcing them, and that therefore the whole concept of a 'human right', as it is commonly used in contemporary political philosophy, is a confusion. This is a profound and concise essay on the basic structure of contemporary politics, written throughout in a voice that is sceptical, engaged, and clear.

RAYMOND GEUSS is Reader in Philosophy at the University of Cambridge. He has taught widely in the United States and Germany, and has been an editor of the series of Cambridge Texts in the History of Political Thought since its inception. His previous books include *The Idea of a Critical Theory* (Cambridge, 1981), *Morality, Culture, and History* (Cambridge, 1999), and *Public Goods, Private Goods* (Princeton, 2001). He has also published a collection of classical verse in his own English translations, *Parrots, Poets, Philosophers, and Good Advice* (London, 1999).

HISTORY AND ILLUSION IN POLITICS

RAYMOND GEUSS

CAMBRIDGE
UNIVERSITY PRESS

CAMBRIDGE UNIVERSITY PRESS
Cambridge, New York, Melbourne, Madrid, Cape Town, Singapore,
São Paulo, Delhi, Dubai, Tokyo

Cambridge University Press
The Edinburgh Building, Cambridge CB2 8RU, UK

Published in the United States of America by Cambridge University Press, New York

www.cambridge.org
Information on this title: www.cambridge.org/9780521000437

First published 2001
Fourth printing 2006

A catalogue record for this publication is available from the British Library

Library of Congress Cataloguing in Publication data
Geuss, Raymond.
History and illusion in politics / Raymond Geuss.
p.   cm.
Includes bibliographical references and index.
ISBN 0-521-80596-1 – ISBN 0-521-00043-2 (pb.)
1. State, The.   2. Liberalism.   3. Democracy.   4. Human rights.   I. Title.
JC11.G48   2001
320′.01 – dc21   2001016171

ISBN 978-0-521-80596-4 Hardback
ISBN 978-0-521-00043-7 Paperback

Transferred to digital printing 2010

Contents

Preface

The following text arises ultimately out of lectures on political philosophy for beginning undergraduates in the Faculties of Social and Political
Sciences and of Philosophy which I have given in a number of variants
here in Cambridge since 1993. Its immediate predecessor, though, was
a set of lectures I gave in German at the University in Frankfurt/M during summer-semester of 1999 under the title 'Traditionselemente des
Liberalismus'. As befits lectures of this kind I aimed at maximal clarity,
immediate intelligibility, and vividness in presenting a general overview
of what I took to be a central strand of argument rather than at subtle-
ty, originality, or exhaustiveness of treatment. I have not attempted to
eradicate all traces of the origin of this text in oral presentation in the
hope that this will allow it to retain some of the advantages of direct-
ness and simplicity. For this reason I have also tried to refrain as much
as possible from engaging with the enormous, and often helpful and
interesting, contemporary literature on political philosophy. My thanks
to Prof. Dr Wolfgang Detel and Prof. Dr Axel Honneth, both of the
Philosophy Faculty of the University of Frankfurt, for the invitation to
Frankfurt and for making my stay there pleasant and instructive.

History and Illusion in Politics may not seem prima facie to be a very obvious equivalent of 'Traditionselemente des Liberalismus' except that I
see 'liberalism' as being the main form of contemporary political theory.
My interest is in the practical coherence of a certain general framework
for orienting political action in the contemporary world. I want to keep
in view at the same time two necessities: the necessity of acting coherently in the political world and the necessity of historical understanding
of our situation. As a general point I hold that philosophy can provide a
practical orientation for politics only if it keeps both of these necessities
in focus. In addition I want to claim in particular that there is a fundamental incoherence in the way we think about politics, in the basic tacit
assumptions made even by those who disagree most radically on most of

the issues that (rightly) concern those in the world of practical everyday politics.

I owe a great debt of gratitude to my colleagues here in Cambridge, who have provided me with an extremely nourishing environment. My most important intellectual debt is to John Dunn, with whom I have had the privilege of conducting regular seminars on political philosophy during the past five or six years; these seminars have been a continuing source of information and enlightenment for me. Hilary Gaskin gave me detailed comments on several drafts of this manuscript which resulted in significant improvements on virtually every page. I also owe particular thanks to Zeev Emmerich, Michael Frede, Peter Garnsey, Lawrence Hamilton, Ross Harrison, Geoff Hawthorn, Anna and Istvan Hont, Susan James, Gareth Stedman Jones, David Runciman, Beverley and David Sedley, Quentin Skinner, Helen Thompson, and Richard Tuck. None of these people is to be construed as in any way responsible for the remaining deficiencies of this work.

Introduction

Human beings are constantly subject to a variety of demands that they act in certain ways. Some of these demands may be ones that present themselves to us as arising (to use an almost unavoidable metaphor) from 'within' ourselves, either directly from our bodily constitution, as when I am cold and wish to warm myself or hungry and wish to eat; or in more highly mediated ways from various long-term projects we hold, as when I wish to read the work of Akhmatova and so must now begin to learn Russian. In addition the various moral or evaluative views we hold may give rise to demands 'from within', as when a decent person refrains from dipping into the unattended till in the shop, or jumping a queue. Sometimes, however, the demands are imposed on me not so much from within as by others. These externally imposed demands are themselves of different types and come from a variety of sources: the Inland Revenue Service invites and requires me to pay out a certain portion of my salary to the Treasury each year in tax (and they will proceed against me through the legal system if I fail to pay), a notice board informs me that the Board of Managers of a certain private club prohibits me from smoking on the club premises (and I will be embarrassed if an officer of the club asks me in front of the assembled members to stop smoking), friends insist that I join them in an expedition and will be very disappointed if I refuse, and so on. All human individuals and groups must act in such a way as to try to attain the goals they have, while negotiating their way through an almost invariably dense thicket of such diverse and, potentially at least, conflicting demands. It is not unreasonable to think that our actions will be more enlightened and successful if we are well informed about the environment in which they take place. 'Practical' (as opposed to 'theoretical') philosophy is devoted to trying to understand the situation of human agents who are confronted with the need to act; political philosophy turns its attention mainly to kinds of collective human action that involve co-operation with or aggression against other groups of human agents. Part of the 'situation' is a knowledge of the more important features of the natural world and the causal laws that govern them; a further part is knowledge of the entities and agencies that make up our social and political world and their properties, including their causal properties: what is the European Union and what does it have the power to do to me? How are multi-national corporations run and how much influence do or can they have on the legislative activity of modern states? Who are the parliamentary representatives for this region, how can I get in touch with them, and what can they really do?

The practical situation, then, includes not only natural and social objects, but also the ideas and conceptions people have. In some situations people do just knock one another about, treating each other as no more than physical bodies or as mere animals, like executioners dragging a condemned man off to his fate or enemies confronting each other in a shell-hole, but one cannot get very far in understanding human life if one thinks of it exclusively on the model of moving objects about or getting highly complex animals to do as one wishes. One major reason for this is that people do not simply wish to act, but they also wish to describe their actions in ways that they and others will find acceptable, to deflect possible criticism, to enlist (ideally) active support for projects they think important, and so on. Doing this requires the use of a historically existing language and appeal to existing human ideas and conceptions. I can perhaps change people's views by speaking with them or acting with or on them, but except in extraordinary circumstances there needs to be enough initial 'human contact' for this process of transformation to get going, and such 'human contact' will operate through an existing language and set of beliefs. These existing conceptions are important in two distinct ways. First, I will myself have certain views about the political world and how it works, how it ideally ought to work, and so on, and these will have an important influence on the way I act. Even minimal reflection will suffice to make me aware that I have not myself invented these conceptions but have taken them over from various people in my environment, who in turn had them from others. When I use 'undemocratic' as a reproach, part of the reason I do so is because I have been subjected to a barrage of speech and writing about 'democracy' and its virtues during all of my conscious life. I do not mean that I feel I have been brainwashed; rather I feel that I have been given a good opportunity to develop proper views on this topic. I also know, however, that if I had lived two hundred years ago, I would almost certainly have followed the then virtually universal use of 'democratic' as a term of reproach.

Thus Kant held that democracy was inherently a form of 'despotism' because in a democracy a majority vote is taken to warrant overriding the vote of any (dissenting) individual, and many of the framers of the United States Constitution were careful to *deny* that the republic they envisaged would be a 'democracy'.[1]

In 'our' time and place, that is, at the beginning of the twenty-first century in Western Europe (and in Europe's ideological dependencies around the world), there are prevailing assumptions about politics and the good society which are no less firmly entrenched in our political life and thought for not always being explicitly expressed. One of the most important of these is an assumption that there is a single ideal model for thinking about politics. This model is the democratic liberal state with a capitalist economy, and a commitment to a set of human rights for its citizens. There are five distinct elements here – liberalism, democracy, the state, the capitalist economy, the doctrine of human rights – but in much contemporary thinking about politics it is tacitly assumed that these five items form a more or less natural, or at any rate minimally consistent and practically coherent, set. I want to suggest – and this is the main thesis of this book – that such an assumption is to a large extent an illusion. The conjunction of these five elements in contemporary Western societies was by no means virtually inevitable or even especially likely, but is rather the result of a highly contingent historical process. Furthermore, if the individual parts that compose this framework are considered carefully, some of them will show themselves to be highly confused or at best only very dubiously coherent, some are extremely implausible, and several can be seen to stand in relations of considerable tension with other elements in the set.

We are familiar with the kind of claim made in the last paragraph – that often the people living at a particular time and place will share a characteristic set of conceptions and assumptions of the kind described. If one wants to understand the politics of an epoch of which this is true, it is argued, it is natural to start by trying to understand that set. It is, however, in my view very important to see exactly what 'shared conceptions' means, and equally important to see what it does not mean. To start with the negative, there is a common way of proceeding which can be found in the work of some historians and which is broadly characteristic of most forms

---

[1] I. Kant, *Zum ewigen Frieden*, 'Zweiter Abschnitt. Erster Definitivartikel zum ewigen Frieden', in *Kant Werkansgabe*, ed. W. Weischedel (Frankfurt/M: Suhrkamp, 1977), vol. XI. See T. Ball, *Transforming Political Discourse* (Oxford: Oxford University Press, 1988), pp. 59–60, 76–8. In the ancient world note Alkibiades' speech to the Spartans in Thucydides VI. 89.

of liberalism, although by no means restricted to liberals. This approach thinks of a society as a moral whole characterised by a single, unitary, consistent underlying conception of the world, morality, and politics. Thus people in sixteenth-century Florence accepted 'The Renaissance World-View', people in late nineteenth-century Britain were 'Victorians', and so on. Often there is then a shift from this purported historical or sociological fact to a series of normative theses which are presented as if they followed simply and directly from this fact, but which are, on the contrary, highly speculative and highly questionable. Although this shift is rarely expressed in so many words, operating rather more frequently by insinuation, one can reconstruct it as involving three steps. First, it is suggested that if two people live in the same society at the same time, they will share many concepts, values, and views. It is an empirical question whether or not this is true in given circumstances, but when it is true, it is true enough. Then from this the conclusion is drawn that such people agree on a coherent central set of substantive moral beliefs that are, at least in principle, capable of being articulated, and that would continue to be felt to be binding by the agents, if they were fully articulated. Finally from this is drawn the conclusion that agents in the society could always, if they wished, and if the conditions were propitious, reach *moral consensus* with each other (because, after all, they 'share the same world-view' at some level).[2]

It is sometimes suggested that liberalism is about the recognition of human variety. This is not false, but it is, I think, a superficial view – only one very small part of the full story, and a highly misleading part, if taken in isolation. Liberals think rather that human societies are *capable of consensus* despite their variety. Arabs and Israelis, Russians and Tchechens, Serbs and Albanians, Tutsis and Hutus, Muslims and Christians may disagree superficially, but they *can* find consensus that will allow them to live together in peace. What is characteristically liberal is the attempt always to see society *sub specie consensus*. This approach, however, is completely misguided. It is not that consensus is inherently a bad thing, but it is such

---

[2] The German philosopher Habermas presents an almost clinically pure instance of this which differs from other versions in two ways. First his version seems to turn on a pun involving the German expression (*sich*) *verständigen* (which can mean either 'understand and make oneself understood to another other person' or 'reach a binding agreement with'). Second he thinks that there are a priori grounds to believe that at the deepest level we *all* – all humans – must share the same world-view, or at any rate must share a commitment to the same set of formal conditions for having a world-view, and thus must all be capable of reaching a universal consensus. See his 'Wahrheitstheorien', in *Wirklichkeit und Reflexion: Festschrift für Walter Schulz* (Pfullingen: Neske, 1973), pp. 252ff. and *Moralbewußtsein und kommunikatives Handeln*. Frankfurt/M: Suhrkamp, 1983, pp. 97–9.

an obscure and elusive concept that one is right to be suspicious of substantive claims that depend too strongly on it. Furthermore it is less clear than is often suggested that consensus in any of the usual and morally laden senses of that term is potentially universal: there simply is less of it around than people often suppose, and there are reasons for suspecting that there are strict limits to how much consensus 'could' be attained in any practically significant sense of the word 'could'. The normative standing even of 'real' existing consensus is not always unproblematic. Those in power obviously have an interest in claiming that a state of affairs which benefits them rests on a stable, morally binding consensus, so one must take their testimony with a grain of salt. In general, the price that would have to be paid for it is often higher than liberals are willing to admit (which does not, of course, imply that it is never reasonable to pay it).

In contrast to the liberal view, Marxists, of course, have always claimed that practically irreconcilable conflict is just as basic to all existing human societies as actual or potential consensus is. Nietzsche adds to this the very astute suggestion that we see 'modern' individuals as inherently guided by *different* and not self-evidently compatible 'moralities', that is, both diverse ways of acting and diverse ways of judging action morally.[3] Conflict exists, that is, not merely between groups but also within each individual as diverse forms of morality struggle for hegemony. No era and no individual has a completely clearly articulated, single consistent world-view. 'What we all share' is usually an overlapping jumble of only half-developed and potentially contradictory views. In nineteenth-century Britain, for instance, people may in one sense have been said to 'have' or 'share' the same world-view in that virtually all of them may have felt the gradual ebb of Christianity and feudal beliefs about status and honour, and the force of utilitarian considerations – but it did not follow that anyone *agreed* with anyone else in any significant or substantive sense. First of all, virtually all of the elements in this mixture were ill-defined – *what* exactly was meant by 'Christian morality' to begin with? – and second there would be no unique recipe according to which the ingredients of the melange had been combined.

Nietzsche views human society *sub specie belli*, although the *bellum* in question need not be conducted with fists, pikestaffs, or missiles but may consist of the genteel exchange of witticisms. Politics is about conflict and disagreement, and this means not only that parties will disagree,

---

3 F. W. Nietzsche, *Jenseits von Gut und Böse* in *Kritische Gesamt-ausgabe*, ed. G. Colli and M. Montinari (Berlin: de Gruyter, 1967ff.), vol. V, § 215.

but also that they will have a motivation to exploit existing conflicts or ambiguities in shared beliefs and values. Thus at certain times and places there might be a widely shared belief that society is naturally hierarchical with a king at the head, and also that there should be an established church. This is compatible with disagreement about who is to be king, what the king's specific powers are, and how the king is to be related to the established church. There may be both genuine and opportunistically dissimulated differences in the conception of what is demanded by reason, custom, decency, prudence, and scripture; there are also, of course, differences in the other values and priorities individual human beings will have, and greatly divergent judgements about the empirical world and the possibilities of human action. All of this will offer fertile ground for discord.

Since the ancient world[4] it has been a commonplace that forms of large-scale 'disagreement', like war, presuppose at least *some* form of internal consensus among the parties in conflict. The troops of country A cannot effectively attack those of country B unless the officers of A have control of their own troops, a control that would be ineffective if it rested on nothing more than brute force. This is sometimes mobilised as an argument in favour of at least a limited priority of consensus. Considerations from the observation of the early development of human infants might also be marshalled in the same cause. It requires no great astuteness to suggest that neither consensus nor conflict is the exclusive basis of human life and history. One has only as much consensus as one has (and no more), and can get only as much as one in fact 'can' get (in specificable senses of 'can') and no more. Standing pools of consensus exist, as do cascades of conflict. Some of the pools are malarial, and many of the cascades are dangerous and destructive. One must approach both with as much care and as much moral scepticism as one deploys anywhere else. Nevertheless I would wish to argue that a focus on conflict and discord has, at least, distinct methodological advantages, given the centrality of disagreement in politics.

In *Zur Genealogie der Moral* Nietzsche develops an approach to history which he calls 'genealogy'.[5] Genealogy starts from a form of historical nominalism. Nietzsche thought that Socrates had put us on the wrong track by suggesting that it was important to try to get formal definitions of those human phenomena that were of the greatest concern to us. It

---

[4] Plato, *Republic*, 351c–352a.

[5] I discuss these methodological views further in my 'Nietzsche and Genealogy', now reprinted in *Morality, Culture, and History* (Cambridge: Cambridge University Press 1999).

was perfectly possible and appropriate, Nietzsche thought, to seek for definitions of abstract items or of features of the natural world. Thus terms like 'triangle', 'water', 'mass', or 'gene' could be defined. The reason this was possible, in Nietzsche's view, was precisely that such terms designated items which were not part of history. A triangle was a triangle in fifth-century Greece or in nineteenth-century Tasmania, and the same was true of water. Human history, though, was concerned in the first instance not with entities such as these, but with objects such as Christianity, punishment, conscience, and morality, which were historically inherently *variable* configurations of powers, functions, structures, and beliefs. These 'objects' were bearers of multiple 'meanings' at any given time, and the constellation of the meanings associated with any one of them was constantly shifting. Incarceration in the twelfth century has a different role, function, and meaning from incarceration in the penal systems of the nineteenth century.[6] Freedom meant something different for Luther, Epictetus, and Herzen. Third-century Christianity was not the same as eighteenth-century Christianity. 'Christianity' – the concept and the reality – is what a succession of humans have made it by virtue of acting in certain ways. In acting people have different goals, changing values, variable interests, and these differences come to be reflected in the shifting meaning of the term. Was Christianity 'really' or 'essentially' Christ's first-century Jewish way of living, the doctrine of Paul, or the decrees on the nature of the Trinity made by a certain church council? Was it inherently a form of liberation from the Law or a highly restrictive discipline of the will? Was Manicheanism a form of Christianity? Was the Inquisition 'Christian'? Was Cistercian architecture particularly Christian? How about the architecture of the Austrian baroque? Or Hagia Sophia (now a mosque)?

In Nietzsche's memorable phrase, only what has no history can be defined. To try to get a single adequate formal definition of Christianity, punishment, liberalism, or democracy is to miss the point. Human words and human institutions are interlaced. Words arise and develop through actual human uses of them in contexts in which power is being exercised in one way or another. Through time human institutions are modified to serve new ends. Each re-use of a word like 'democracy' or 'Christianity' in a new context is potentially a reinterpretation of it. There are no 'natural' or unbreakable limits to the ways in which such reinterpretation can take place. What one must understand in dealing with

---

[6] See M. Foucault, *Surveiller et punir* (Paris: Gallimard, 1975).

phenomena like Christianity or the state is a history, that is, a precise way in which through the course of time institutions and words have evolved under the pressure of the conflicting demands put on them by individuals and groups of humans, the natural world, and other institutions. This is not a reductivist view which claims that the ideas people associate with Christianity, the penal system, and other such things are 'mere' epiphenomena – a view held by some vulgar Marxists. Rather it is the view that beliefs, words, thoughts, intentions, and concepts are absolutely essential because without them and the 'meanings' they help humans impose on the world there would be no Christianity to study. At the same time, however, the beliefs that Christians hold in any given era are only *part* of the full story of Christianity. One can make a map or get a systematic overview of different forms of Christianity using 'empirical' ('historical' in the Greek sense) methods, but there is no analytic short-cut, no Royal Road (or Kantian *Heerstraße*) which bypasses history and yet leads to any significant understanding. Concepts, then, at any rate those which refer to human phenomena, are usually historically accumulated constellations of rather heterogeneous elements.

The Nietzschean view I have just sketched seems to undermine the claim which I earlier described as 'the main thesis of this book' in two respects. First, if virtually *all* world-views are historically contingent conjunctions of ill-defined concepts and half-unarticulated theoretical fragments, then it is no particular indictment of 'our' model of political life that it has that property. Second, if the concepts we actually use in politics are irremediably fuzzy and open-textured, and we can shape and warp them in indeterminately flexible ways to suit our purposes, then what exactly is the concern about coherency? The pragmatist variant of this second objection is that it is a mistake in any case to worry too much about the general coherence of theoretical structures. If theories are like tools, then the only useful question to ask about them is how well they do a particular job in the particular context in which their employment is envisaged. Abstract speculation about the 'coherence' or 'incoherence' of different tools is inherently otiose.

As far as the first of these is concerned, it is true that I see it as no objection to our current political views that they are a historical jumble. It is, however, an 'objection' if we suffer from the illusion that it is *not* such a jumble. Do we, however, suffer from this illusion? Is it really news to us that our concepts have a history and that they do not all fit together like the parts of a jigsaw puzzle? It is true that if one were to ask some of the most profound and astute political thinkers of the past century in their most reflective moments, they would admit *individually* about some or even each of my five items (liberalism, the state, the concept of rights, democracy, capitalism) that it had a history, and they would also admit that the conjunction of the five was to some extent the result of particular historical processes which could have had a different outcome. I think that many would also admit that in individual cases there might be some tensions between, say, democracy and liberalism. However, there is a difference between admitting *isolated* forms of historical contingency and conflict, and seeing the whole array of these five items as systematically in conflict. There is also a distinction between the individual insights some elite theorists might catch a fleeting glimpse of and express in moments of special reflection, and their actual ability to think through the consequences of these momentary illuminations fully and embody them systematically in their everyday practice as theorists. There is a difference again between either of these things and the commonly shared political beliefs of relatively unreflective ordinary people. Few people have been able to keep a very firm general grip on the insight that some of the elements of our most deeply held political beliefs are angular, misshapen, brittle, riven with cracks and none too sturdy or stable in themselves, and very ill suited to each other. Getting such a firm grip, I suggest, might change our political practice for the better. Similarly, the fact that we will never succeed in reducing our political views and our world-view to the aesthetically pleasing state of the Code Napoléon or a textbook on mathematics is no argument for failing to try to get as clear about it as we can.

As far as the second objection is concerned, one can turn the pragmatist argument around. The various political conceptions that are under discussion in this text are not mere speculations, but rather tools for guiding action. It is a matter of some practical importance whether or not a certain state is accepted as legitimate and admitted to the United Nations, whether or not legal rights of a certain type are recognised and, if they are, how they are enforced. Even liberal views about toleration and human autonomy are intended to direct us towards certain modes of political action; such views have had a very significant impact in the real world in which we live. Precisely for this reason it is perfectly reasonable to ask, whatever one thinks about the philosophical status of concepts, whether one can *act* on all of these political views together in a coherent way.

If I want to minimise the extent to which I am the mere plaything of a historical and social process over which I have no control, one of the things I will do is reflect and try to give myself an account of the basic conceptions that underlie my view of the social and political world. Among other things, it is, then, perfectly reasonable for me to ask where these conceptions come from, what shape they have, and in what contexts it makes sense to try to act on them. Although concepts are flexible they are not *tabulae rasae*. They carry their history with them. This history does not strictly determine how they must be used, but it does affect to a very significant extent how easy or how difficult it will be to modify them, changing their meaning and reference in one direction rather than another. There are limits to how far one can actually succeed in reflecting and probably even more narrowly set limits to the extent to which one can gain any control. We can never absolutely free ourselves from history and attain an absolutely clear and coherent set of action-orienting views about our political world. It does not follow from this – and it seems self-evidently false – that we are no better off in any respect when we are enlightened about our concepts and theories than when we were not.

I take it that it is in the spirit of Nietzsche to hold that as human beings, or at any rate as specifically *modern* human beings, we are in-eluctably caught between two contrary impulses. One the one hand, we unavoidably desire to get as much conceptual control over the major areas of our lives as we can. This is the origin of our attempt to attain a unitary systematic overview. The traditional 'definition' was the vehicle of this attempt. On the other hand, once one has fully felt the force of the Nietzschean insight that such definition is impossible, there is no forgetting or going back. If neither of these two impulses is to be denied, the process of continuing to try to 'define' while concretely recognising the limits and the failure of any such attempt is a continuous one in all theoretical enquiries that have a historical component. It is the very stuff of the history of politics and of political thought.

Some may think that in my general account of our political world-view I have left out a sixth element which is of great importance: the state in the modern world, they will claim, is conceived as a nation-state. Nationalism is undoubtedly a significant force in contemporary politics, and not merely in backward places. Recognising this, however, is compatible with thinking that 'the nation' is not of much value as an analytic tool and does not designate a fundamental dimension of politics. In this, as in so much else, it seems to me that Max Weber points us in the right direction.[7] Weber was very concerned to reject a certain nineteenth-century view which held that we can look at the earth and pick out the 'nations' by

---

[7] Max Weber, *Wirtschaft und Gesellschaft* (Tübingen: Mohr, 1956), pp. 527f., cf. also p. 242.

reference to empirical properties independently of the existing forms of political organisation (for instance, by language, family relations, religion, birth, etc.), and then ask which of these 'nations' has its own nation-state. In contrast to this view, he held that 'nation' is not really a concept like the usual empirical concepts employed by sociologists, that is, a mental construct that merely grouped together a series of empirical properties. Rather, he thought, 'nation' inherently expressed a certain value judgement. That is, 'X and Y belong to the same nation' was not a claim that had a standing like 'X and Y have hair of the same colour'. Rather it was a claim like 'Work of art X and work of art Y are both immature products of artists who later became masters.' By denying that a 'nation' is a normal empirical concept Weber did not mean to deny the obvious fact that we can unproblematically categorise de Gaulle as a Frenchman and Joschko Fischer as a German. Nor did he mean simply to refer to the well-known fact that one cannot find necessary and sufficient empirical conditions for determining what is and what is not a nation. Co-natality, consanguinity, uniformity of religion, language – none of these empirical features will do the discriminatory trick. This in itself might not seem very striking because, if my general line of argument is correct, one can rarely ever find necessary and sufficient empirical conditions – a 'definition' – of important political concepts. 'Nation', then, seems no worse than anything else. What Weber means by calling 'nation' a value-concept is that using the term 'nation' is expressing a demand on the social world: that membership in a certain group, characterised in a certain way, *ought to* give rise to feelings of solidarity and positive identification with other members of the group, and that these feelings should be of a kind that would in principle lead to some potential form of collective action. The way the group is picked out – the features thought to justify including some persons as a members and excluding others – will vary, and the form of solidarity which is demanded will also vary historically. Thus the medieval University of Paris was the centre of higher education for the whole of Western Europe, drawing students not just from 'France' but also from the British Isles, the Pannonian Plains, Iberia, and so on. The *nationes* were groups of students from the same geographic region who clubbed together to get the benefit of collective living arrangements. What counted as 'the same geographic area' was only very crudely defined, but the form of solidarity expected was clear. To say you were a member of the *natio teutonica* meant that by virtue of coming from east of the Rhine you were potentially a contributor to and beneficiary of such a student dormitory/fraternity. Since the nineteenth century, however,

Weber claims, the concrete form '(national) solidarity' can be expected to take is one that is inherently political. Claims to membership in the same 'nation' are tacitly demands for membership in the same political association. Since the state is the main form of political organisation in the modern world claims about who belongs to what nation are really demands about where the boundaries of states should (ideally) run. To say that two persons belong to the same 'nation' is to say that you think they ought (ideally) to belong to the same state. This does not mean that at an individual level a particular nation does not exist until brought into being by an appropriate state. The claim is not that there is no Czech nation until there is a Czech state. There was no Czech state until the twentieth century, but one can perfectly reasonably speak of the Czech nation in the nineteenth century. The claim rather is that to think in the nineteenth century of the Czech nation would have been tacitly to demand that all people having certain properties – for example, born in a certain place and/or speaking a certain language – should feel a very particular kind of solidarity with each other. This 'solidarity' was stipulatively specified in the following way: all Czechs should join together in certain socio-economic arrangements, the appropriate embodiment of which in the political realm is an autonomous modern state. The Czech state need not predate the Czech nation, but the modern general idea 'nation' is conceptually parasitic on the modern idea of the state. For these reasons 'nation' does not seem to me to deserve a place among the central items of our political world-view.

A full genealogy of contemporary political thought would be a work which discussed in appropriate detail the history and origin of contemporary political terms and theories and set this in the context of power struggles between individuals, institutions, and social movements in the recent past. It would be a fuller and better genealogy, the more detailed and illuminating an account it could give and the further back it could reach. My own mode of procedure in this manuscript is not really that of 'genealogy', but more like that of traditional analytic philosophy: the distinction of senses of terms, especially in argumentative contexts, and the discussion of what can be done with them. For a variety of reasons, I will not discuss the capitalist economic formation separately, but will treat successively the state, liberalism, democracy, and human rights. I do not see 'genealogical' inquiry as excluding standard forms of analytic philosophy (especially not to conceptual analysis, as it used to be practised), nor do I see it as an alternative to historical treatment. Nietzsche himself, as any careful reading of *Zur Genealogie der Moral* will confirm, was a deft practitioner of conceptual analysis; after all, one of the central insights of *Zur Genealogie der Moral* is that the concept 'good' has two distinct contraries ('bad' and 'evil'). Nietzsche's particular interest in historical philology as a potential philosophical tool is also well documented.[8] I see genealogy as complementary to both historical scholarship and analytic philosophy, as putting analysis in its appropriate wider context, one in which it gains historical and political substance, and as giving to historical discussion a point it might otherwise not obviously have.

I have given this book the title *History and Illusion in Politics* because I am convinced that there is a sense in which the study of history can help us to free ourselves from certain illusions to which we would otherwise be subject. This work is, then, not a history *of* politics, or even a systematic history *of* concepts that are used in politics. 'History' in the title is rather intended to refer to my claim that reflection on history can be politically enlightening.

---

[8] See, for instance, the *Anmerkung* at the end of Essay One of *Zur Genealogie der Moral*, in *Kritische Gesamt-ausgabe*, ed. G. Colli and M. Montinari (Berlin: de Gruyter, 1967 ff.), vol. v.

CHAPTER I

The state

1. POLITICAL ASSOCIATIONS

In the contemporary world the term 'politics' is used sometimes very expansively, and sometimes in a more restricted way. Thus, we speak, on the one hand, of 'the politics of the family', 'office politics', 'bio-politics', 'gender-politics', etc., but then also more narrowly of politics as referring specifically to the struggle for election to the great offices of the state, attempts to influence the way in which the power of the state is wielded, and so on. Weber has this contrast in mind when he distinguishes a 'narrower' notion of politics from a wider one. The 'narrower' notion understands politics as that which has to do with the acquisition, distribution, and exercise of state power. The wider notion sees politics as having to do with any set of relations of subordination, that is of command on the one side and obedience on the other, even if these do not take place in the framework of a state or draw on the resources of the state.[1] We might think that *both* of these two Weberian conceptions are actually too narrow to encompass all the things we sometimes mean when we speak of politics. State-power is in the last analysis coercive power, and commanding is not the only way in which one person can get others to act in a certain way. There is also a realm within which the phenomena of persuasion, influence, and emulation are found. In small, voluntary, egalitarian groups that were detached from the structures of state-power, for instance in a chess club, there might be disagreement about means and goals, discussion, the formation of parties, jockeying for place, and in short many of the things which we would reasonably call constituents of 'a politics'. This 'political' activity might, however, operate without recourse to force, state-power, or a kind of subordination that could correctly be described as relations of command and obedience. No one in the chess club really 'commands' anyone else to do anything. There is,

[1] Max Weber, '*Politik als Beruf*', in *Gesammelte politische Schriften* (Tübingen: Mohr, 1980), pp. 505–7.

one might argue, a third and widest sense of politics in which it designates simply the process of influencing people and getting things done (in one way or another) in the realm of collective human action.

Although it is extremely important to keep in mind that the term 'politics' is used to refer to a wide dimension of human social life rather than simply to struggles about the disposition over state-power, there seems little doubt that the modern state is one of the most important features of the space within which politics in all senses now takes place in the modern world. In view of this it makes sense, in trying to understand politics, to start with the state.

Perhaps the most widely influential traditional approach to understanding the state is one initiated by Max Weber at the turn of the twentieth century.[2] His approach is broadly functional in that he defines the state as that which performs a certain activity successfully. A society, he argues, is organised as a state (or a state exists) where there is a successful monopolisation of the exercise of legitimate violence. It is this function or activity that is central; 'the state' is simply whatever agency it is that discharges that function (successfully).

When Weber is being most careful, he distinguishes clearly between 'a state' and what he calls 'a political association'; he gives a conceptually genetic account of these two concepts by building them up gradually from simpler notions. The progression from 'association' to 'political association' to 'state' is intended as a conceptual or analytic one, and its relation to history is intentionally left unspecified. The basic notion from which Weber starts is that of what he calls an 'association' (*Verband*). This, for Weber, is a social group which satisfies two conditions. First, it exhibits a certain continuing order, which results from the fact that the members of the group follow a certain set of rules; an 'association' differs from a random or accidental assemblage of persons. One can reasonably doubt that any thing we would be at all interested in calling a 'social' grouping would fail to meet this condition. The second condition an 'association' must satisfy is that there must be a designated agent, or group of agents, who is specifically charged with maintaining the order the group exhibits, that is, with seeing that the rules are observed. I will call these designated agents 'Overseers' and will usually assume for the purposes of simplicity of exposition that there are several of them, although in principle there could be a single Overseer.

---

[2] I follow closely the account given in 'Politik als Beruf', pp. 505–20, and *Wirtschaft und Gesellschaft*, pp. 1–30.

Thus a group of people which meets 'informally' every Tuesday in the park of some European city to play chess does not necessarily form what Weber calls an 'association' just by virtue of the fact that they follow certain rules (the rules of chess). They do not form an 'association' even if they agree among themselves formally on a set of highly specific further *ad hoc* rules that will govern *their* play and that are distinct from the usually accepted rules of chess (such as that the person sitting closest to a certain tree always takes white). They fail to constitute an association by virtue of lacking Overseers, a particular person (or group of people) whose job it is to ensure that the rules are obeyed and thus the established order maintained. This is, as I said, a kind of idealised analysis introduced for the purposes of clarifying a certain concept. In the case described in the text, the members of the group of chess players would *also* be expected to be members of a political association (in Weber's sense). That is, there would be municipal or national police around to enforce *some* of the rules that governed their interaction, such as that no one was physically to assault another. Weber, however, would distinguish between the group in question as a 'group of chess players' and the group as a 'group of citizens' (for instance). We are interested *here* in the group as a group of chess players.

At this point in the analysis Weber intentionally leaves a number of questions open: how the Overseers are appointed (by election, birth, informal usurpation which is not questioned, etc.), whether or not membership in the association is voluntary, how persons become members (whether by a free act of accession, by birth, by co-optation, by sortition, or in some other way), whether or not the Overseers are members of the group, and what means the Overseers use or may use to ensure that the rules are obeyed. The question of the possible legitimacy or illegitimacy of the Overseers and of the way in which the Overseers exercise power is also left open. That Weber leaves so many of these questions open is important for a number of reasons, in particular because those who are not members of the group may not be expected to conform to the rules they enforce. In principle a casual passer-by or *kibbitzer* who might not even actively play chess (and therefore *a fortiori* will not be bound in acting by many of the rules of the game), may appear, stop to watch, and gradually become recognised as one of the Overseers. Such a person may by the use of highly informal means (e.g. pointing out attempted violations in a loud sarcastic voice) succeed in maintaining order. To the extent to which this occurs, an 'association' exists.

We speak of a *specifically* 'political association' (and not just of an 'association' *tout court*) when the Overseers have at their disposal one very particular means of enforcing order and conformity to the rules: the use or threat of physical force, violence, or coercion. It is this threat of the use of force which, for Weber, makes an association 'political'. For this reason Weber would reject the third and widest of the three senses of 'politics' which were distinguished above. Where the possible use of force is not at issue, there is no politics, strictly speaking.

It is not, to be sure, that a 'political association' always or characteristically or even regularly employs force to get things done or that politics is always a matter of the explicit threat to use force. In fact, Weber thinks that societies have a natural tendency to replace the use of force, which is inefficient, with other indirect forms of control and inducement, so that the more developed the society, the less direct overt use of force there will be in it. Nevertheless 'the political' refers to a domain in which the use of force *as a final resort* is always present as a real possibility.[3] To speak of fully peaceful forms of persuasion as political is to speak of them relative to their possible effect on the possibility of coercive action. The governing body of a private club that is formed within a modern state can perhaps exclude me from membership in the club if I violate specific rules or make a general nuisance of myself; they may bar me from entering the club-house, and deprive me of honours, privileges, and benefits they have bestowed on me, but they cannot break my leg, tie me up, or even threaten (seriously) to do either of these things. 'Cannot' in this context means that if they try to assault me I can appeal to the police to prevent their action or punish them, and that I assume that under normal circumstances this is sufficient to deter the officers of the club from doing anything drastic. I am assuming in this example that the club is embedded in a wider, effective political association. That the officers of the club may not use violence in enforcing the rules is what is meant by saying that a club is not *per se* a 'political' organisation in the relevant sense.

If we do call a given club a political organisation, it is not by virtue of its own internal properties but by virtue of the role it may play in the acquisition and influencing of power in a wider specifically political domain in which force is potentially used. We might, that is, call a given club a political organisation despite the fact that it does not enforce its own rules through the use of violence if, for instance, the ministers of a modern state informally use the club as a place to meet, discuss pending (potentially coercive) legislation or policy, and form alliances in private.

---

3 Weber calls it the '*ultima ratio* when other means fail' (*Wirtschaft und Gesellschaft*, p. 29).

In this case non-ministerial members of the club might have what could be considered to be an inappropriate chance to influence government policy and ministers who were not part of the club might be thought to be inappropriately disadvantaged. The club would count as political by virtue of its role in influencing the distribution of power in the state.

Weber adds to the above account a further condition which is odd and not finally analytically useful, but which points in the direction of an important issue, namely, he states that a political association is one which maintains its order 'within a given geographic area continuously'. One might wonder whether the addition of a specific reference to a given fixed geographic area is warranted, that is, whether it contributes to cutting up the conceptual space in a useful way. We are accustomed to assume that the basic political entities will be geographically fixed and located, and that they will be temporally continuous. In principle, though, one could speak of a social order that was enforced through the threat of coercion by Overseers and that was specified as binding on a group of *people*, for instance on the members of a nomadic tribe, the descendants of certain people, the carriers of certain genes, or the employees of a certain corporation, rather than by reference to a geographic area. Similarly we could imagine seasonally based forms of political power, for instance religious–military commands in primitive agricultural societies that came into effect every summer at the beginning of the campaigning season, and then lapsed until the next year.

Conceptually the condition of geographical fixity and temporal continuity might seem to be simply a contamination of Weber's investigation by relatively superficial features of recent European history. This condition, however, although conceptually contingent, is not utterly groundless. The main kind of rule a political association is to enforce is one against physical violence directed by one person against another. Given, then, that physical proximity was for a long time one of the preconditions for the exercise of direct violence against persons, it did make sense to have rules for regulating such violence which were defined for specific geographic areas, and continuous time-periods. If the world were set up so that by hitting you lightly on the side of the head with a hammer I left you unaffected, but gave all members of your immediate family a cerebral haemorrhage several days later, regardless of where they happened to be (Tasmania, Novosibirsk, or Saloniki), geographic definitions of the extent of a political association might not seem so obviously desirable. The same might be true if what we wanted to regulate was telephone conversations; in that case the crucial distinctions would be who was on which exchange, rather than who was physically where. This discussion does, however, draw our attention to what is a very important general issue, namely the boundaries of a political association.

Geographic boundaries with temporal continuity are convenient, so overwhelmingly convenient that we can let their inclusion in the definition pass unchallenged, but there is another set of boundaries that is even more crucial for understanding politics. This is the question of what kinds of human behaviour are considered to fall within the purview of the rules which define the association, that is, how extensive and how detailed a set of rules is enforced, and what domains of human life they cover.

Human groups, after all, vary very significantly in *how much* of life they subject to regulation. Chess clubs do not usually have rules about the diet their members are to follow, and now most universities have ceased to regulate the religious life of their students. Even human political groups of the kind Weber calls 'political associations' differ widely as regards what kind of behaviour they attempt to enforce. We are used to highly extensive, efficient, and sophisticated political associations which have rules regulating very many domains of human life and which try to enforce these rules, but it is important to realise that the scope of the 'rules' which constitute a political association can be much less restrictive and much less encompassing than that.

Looking back from the perspective of such contemporary forms of political organisation, which at least theoretically and in imagination could encompass *all* aspects of human life, we are often surprised to see how limited older legal codes are in their scope, and how much random activity, even random violence, older societies contained and made no attempt to regulate. It is indeed probably incorrect to say that they 'tolerated' such unregulated activity because that falsely suggests the assumption that all behaviour *should* be regulated, and it is just this assumption which seems lacking. Older societies did not actually have the means to enforce regulation over a wide area of human life, but for whatever reason it also seems never to have occurred to at least some of them to try.[4] Thus many societies make a clear distinction between a killing carried out in broad daylight in a public place which the perpetrator makes no attempt to hide, and 'murder', that is, a secret killing (at night, from ambush, in a deserted place, etc.) for which no one publicly announces responsibility.

---

[4] Even 'religion' as at least potentially encompassing *all* of human life seems to be a rather late human invention. Cf. Jan Assmann, *Moses the Egyptian* (Cambridge, Mass.: Harvard University Press, 1998).

A political association between a group of people could be constituted by their joint acceptance of a rule that no 'murder' (secret killing of one member of the group by another) is to be tolerated, and by the institution of an Overseer to enforce this rule. A public killing in broad daylight (or of a human who was not a member of the group) might be thought to be none of the affair of the Overseers, but rather something that is to be left to the vengeance of the individual kinship groups involved (or to the gods). We think we can see why such a system might have a tendency to expand the system of rules to cover more and more areas of human life, just as we have seen that there would be reason to consolidate the system in a compact geographic area, but a tendency of this kind, if it in fact exists, is a relatively superficial and contingent historical matter, not something rooted in any very deep necessity.

Part of the reason for emphasising this point is that we are used to trying to make sense of modern politics through reference to a view, put with great energy by Benjamin Constant,[5] that in ancient societies the 'public powers' interfered with the private lives of citizens – through sumptuary laws, highly restrictive regulation of marriage, inheritance, and commerce, controls on the formation of voluntary associations – much more extensively than would be thought acceptable in modern Western societies. In one sense this is correct, but it is also true that a wide range of things which in the modern world would be regulated by the public authorities (the domestic disciplining of wives, slaves, and children) were not in the ancient world considered part of the public political order and were thus not coercively regulated by the overseeing institutions. Whether or not one whipped one's own slave was not something that belonged to the realm of human action which was covered by the rules which constituted this kind of political association. Ancient societies may have recognised no limit in principle to political intervention, but they also *in fact* had a much more limited notion of what constituted part of the 'public' order than most modern Western societies have. In addition, of course, ancient societies, lacking as they did surveillance equipment, passport controls, DNA profiling, etc., were infinitely more limited in the extent to which they actually *could* intervene in human life. There was not just a smaller private sphere in the ancient world, as a naive reading of Constant might suggest, but there was a different division altogether.

---

[5] See his 'De l'esprit de conquête et de l'usurpation' (originally 1814) and 'De la liberté des anciens comparée à celle des modernes' (1819), both in Constant, *De la liberté chez les modernes*, ed. M. Gauchet (Paris: Hachette, 1980).

2. VIOLENCE, COERCION, AND POWER

'Violence' is to be distinguished on the one hand from coercion and on the other from power. 'Violence' is, I will claim, best understood by focusing on adverbial expressions such as 'to act violently'. Violence, that is, refers to a particular *way* of acting or operating. I act 'violently' if I inflict pain on other humans, or if I act in a way that *would* inflict physical pain or injury on others, were they to happen to be in the path of the action in question. If I strike you, I am acting violently, but I can also be said to be behaving violently if I lash out with my fists in a way that would pain or physically injure you, were they to come into contact with you. This would remain true even if you had prudently moved out of the line of fire. 'Violence' (as a noun) is simply any activity that is conducted violently or considered as an instance of an action performed violently. It is, therefore, not a term that directs any particular attention to the specifically teleological dimension of human action; it has little to do with whether or not any actual end is attained, or indeed even whether or not anyone is trying or intending to achieve an end. If I am blind drunk, I can behave violently without having any very coherent intentions, or at any rate without intending by that behaviour to injure anyone in particular. The 'violence' of the action may also be independent of there being any other person around who is in fact pained by my action. The action is violent because it is the kind of action which, *if* someone else were to be in its way, would result in pain or physical injury.

In contrast to this, 'coercion', I will claim, is not best understood by reference to an adverbial usage, but rather by reference to a verb. I act violently (or, perhaps, I 'use' violence), but I 'coerce you *to do* [something]'. I wish to suggest further that it is more enlightening to look at the transaction between Mabel who coerces and Ethel who is coerced (to do something) initially from the point of view of the victim/object rather than from that of the subject. That is, the hermeneutically basic form is: 'You/he/she/they have coerced (or, "forced") me to do X' or 'You have made me do X', where that means that I have been left with no alternative but to do X, and the reason for this is something you have done. Ethel may perfectly justifiably claim that Mabel is coercing her – leaving her with no alternative but to do X – although Mabel with equal plausibility claims not to be intending anything of the sort. If Ethel is intensely allergic to roses, she may be forced to leave the room when Mabel enters with a large bouquet and sits down beside her. That Ethel leaves the room may even be directly contrary to Mabel's intention in acting.

Similarly Mabel may intend and try to coerce Ethel, and yet fail. Claims about coercion can be made relatively independently of the intentions of the agent who is the purported subject.

As my example of the drunk shows, I can act violently without coercing you to do anything: my random lashing out with my fists is violent, but might be so unfocused that you need not take any account of it. I can even act violently in your general direction without that violence being sufficiently competently executed to cause me to depart in any non-trivial way from the course of action on which I was already embarked. Equally, I can coerce you without using violence. If you are in a small room with two doors I can force you to leave by door A, by locking door B. It seems hard to construe locking a door as an act of 'violence', but it certainly has the result that you have no alternative but to use door B.

Although 'to coerce' means 'to leave with no alternative but X', what counts as having 'no alternative' is highly context-dependent. 'No alternative' usually means 'no reasonable alternative'. To say that locking door B forces you to use door A does not literally mean that you have no alternative but to use door A, because, as the Stoics were fond of pointing out, you probably have the alternative of staying in the room indefinitely. To be sure, if you stay in the room indefinitely, you will probably die of thirst there after a few days. Since this is not a 'reasonable' alternative, given what we know about human nature and normal human preferences, we call it 'no' alternative. If (slow or quick) death is the only alternative to some course of action, it does seem reasonable to say we have no choice. In most cases, however, what will count as 'reasonable' depends very much on circumstances, and in particular on people's beliefs and preferences. One highly sophisticated (but exceedingly difficult) way of controlling populations is by changing what they consider to be 'reasonable' alternatives.

'Power' is used in a number of ways. In the first sense it designates any ability to do something, including abilities of non-human agents. Thus I can say, 'I have the power of speech', or 'This motor has the power of ten horses.' Many people, however, have thought that a more sharply focused notion of power is more appropriate and useful in social and political agency. Thus Bertrand Russell defines power as 'production of intended effect', that is, (my) 'power' as '(my) ability to get what I want'.[6] Because of the reference to what an agent, that is, some human being or corporation, wants, power in this sense designates specifically human

---

[6] B. Russell, *Power: A New Social Analysis* (London: Allen & Unwin, 1938), chapter 3.

abilities. Yet, on the one hand, I may systematically get what I want without having anything we would independently want to call 'power' – as Brian Barry has pointed out, I may be systematically lucky[7] – and on the other hand I may have what seems to the external observer a lot of power without necessarily getting what I want. Much depends on how one interprets 'what I want'.

It is important to avoid two complementary mistakes about the human agent as a being who has wants, preferences, and desires. On the one hand, a Humean conception of human wants as inherently atomistic is highly misleading. A human agent is not a disconnected bundle of completely disparate wants and desires, all of which stand on the same level with each other, and each of which differs from any other only in its intensity and particular object in the external world. Rather I have a set or system of wants that is structured, organised, and nested. To say that my wants are usually structured means (among other things) that I desire various things *as* means to various further things or as constituents of various further things. My wanting them to some extent depends on my having certain beliefs about how they relate to other things I want. On the other hand, my wants and desires do not form a closed, conscious, and fully articulated formal system. My wants are not all always fully articulated, and they change, sometimes exogenously, sometimes as a result of reflection, and sometimes without my being fully aware of it. Their structuring is not necessarily complete in that I am not necessarily always fully conscious of how certain of my desires may relate to others, what reasons I may have for having a certain desire, or indeed whether I have any reason for it at all.

In the present context it is the first of these two properties, the non-atomistic nature of human desire, that is relevant. Hitler did not just want to annexe Austria, dismantle Czechoslovakia, invade Poland, and ensure lasting hegemony over Central Europe, but rather he wanted to invade Poland *in order to* ensure continuing hegemony over Central Europe. It would be a mistake to think that because he was not able to get what he wanted (lasting hegemony over Central Europe) he did not have much power.

The mistake implicit in the claim that Hitler was not powerful *because* he did not get what he wanted, German hegemony over Europe, is familiar in its outlines from Plato's *Gorgias*.[8] In that dialogue Plato argues

---

[7] B. Barry, 'Is it better to be powerful or lucky?', in *Democracy and Power* (Oxford: Oxford University Press, 1991).
[8] Plato, *Gorgias*, 466–81.

the counterintuitive claim that a tyrant really has no power, because to have power is to be able to get what one really wants. Everyone (by general agreement) really wants to be happy, but if, as Plato thinks, to be happy is to be in a harmonious psychic state, and if, as Plato assumes, tyrants are never in a harmonious psychic state, then despite the fact that tyrants can do any number of things, they do not have real power. This argument moves to the conclusion that only the good person, and perhaps only the philosophically enlightened good person, has any real power at all; this conclusion is sufficiently self-evidently false to alert almost any unbiased reader to the fact that there must be at least one fallacy in the argument. The idea that to have power is to be able to get what one really wants is one such fallacy.

Weber construes 'power' even more narrowly than Russell as one's ability to realise one's will even against opposition (no matter what that ability depends on).[9] Weber's idea seems to arise in the context of trying to distinguish between 'power' on the one hand and things like 'influence' on the other. Russell's definition would seem to construe power inclusively in a way that would include the effective employment of influence as an instance of the exercise of power. One might think, though, that although my 'influence' could decide an issue when the others concerned had no special interest in one outcome rather than another, influence reached its limits when it encountered real 'opposition'. Weber's definition is sufficient to distinguish having power from merely using force in that the final component of the definition ('no matter what that ability depends on') explicitly leaves open the possibility that I may have non-violent or non-coercive modes of realising my will, for instance I may have at my disposal reliable techniques (e.g. bribery, deception) which allow me to attain my ends in legislative assemblies even against the will of a certain group of people. The question is whether the use of such techniques can finally be distinguished from forms of 'influence', and what exactly is meant by 'against opposition' or 'against the will' of others. These questions seem to a large extent terminological.

There are, however, two objections to this Weberian approach that do not turn on merely terminological issues. Both of these two objections take up the second of the two properties of the human subject of desire – the lack of full stability, closure, and systematicity in human wanting.[10]

First, Weber's usage seems to presuppose a rather crude model of the exercise of power which may not be inappropriate in some contexts, but

[9] Weber, *Wirtschaft und Gesellschaft*, p. 28.
[10] See above, p. 23.

is not sufficiently differentiated and sophisticated to cover all cases. It is, therefore, not acceptable as a general way of thinking about power. This way of thinking applies to cases in which there are two clearly defined individuals or groups, each of which has a clear will, or desire, or preference about some state of affairs. Sometimes, to be sure, this is a relevant description of the situation. Suppose I am very strong and you are very weak. I want your money but you do not want to give it to me. Since I am strong, however, I can realise my will even against your resistance. In many cases, however, and in by no means the least important, the people involved in a relation of power will not antecedently have clearly articulated preferences; their preferences will rather be inchoate, contradictory, or unformed. If your overwhelming power over me is a stable fact of the environment, this may be an important factor in skewing the very formation of my preferences. The term that is often used of this phenomenon is 'adaptive preference formation'.[11] Humans do not like frustration, and the mechanism of such preference formation works to prevent a state in which my preferences are continually frustrated by preventing me from even developing such preferences, so the role power will play is not so importantly (and certainly not exclusively) that of allowing you to get what you want even against my wishes, but rather that of preventing me from even developing wishes of a certain kind. This phenomenon is even more striking and important in cases in which there is extreme predominance of power on the one side, and relatively little possibility for the person with less power to escape interaction, and in which the inferior has relatively undeveloped and highly plastic preferences. An example of this is the case of parents in long-term interactions with children. In cases like this you may reasonably be said to have a power over me that does not consist in your ability to *overcome* my resistance, but in your ability to prevent me from ever being in a position to articulate desires and interests that would motivate me to put up resistance.[12]

Second, even an adult with well-formed preferences will not just be a bundle of simple preferences about states of the world, but a complex hierarchy of first-order, second-order, and perhaps higher-order preferences, many of them less than fully stable.[13] I may want to drink another glass of wine, but also, knowing that I have had enough, wish I did not

---

[11] J. Elster, *Sour Grapes: Studies in the Subverstion of Rationality* (Cambridge: Cambridge University Press, 1983), esp. chapter 3.
[12] See S. Lukes, *Power: A Radical View* (London: Macmillan, 1974), for further discussion.
[13] See H. Frankfurt, 'Freedom of the Will and the Concept of a Person', now reprinted in his *The Importance of What We Care About* (Cambridge: Cambridge University Press, 1988).

want another glass of wine. I might wish to hit my neighbour, because of something he did which mildly inconvenienced me, but also wish I did not have the wish to do something I think morally reprehensible. In addition, a mature human will have '*prima facie* preferences' and 'all-things-considered preferences'. That is, I may have preferences about features of a situation if these features are presented abstractly and in isolation, but also a perhaps very different set of preferences when I take account of *all* aspects of a given concrete situation. Thus I prefer red wine to white wine (*prima facie*), but, all things considered, on some occasions I may prefer a good and inexpensive white wine to an overpriced mediocre red. Even if I have relatively clear, formed, and fixed *prima facie* preferences (a state of affairs which might well, as I have just said, not hold), it may still be the case that the existence of an enduring relation of power may skew my all-things-considered preferences in a number of ways. This phenomenon is of great political importance, most obviously perhaps in the cases of small countries situated near large and powerful ones (i.e. the Poland-syndrome).

If this account of power is roughly correct, power is clearly different from violence because I can have power by virtue of being able to attain my ends through bribery or manipulation, and bribery is not a form of infliction of physical injury. Equally I can be very violent (for example, when drunk) without having the power to do much of anything, certainly not anything that requires human concentration. If I can coerce you to do X, I have the power to bring X about, but if my power to effect X rests on ability to bribe you, this is not usually thought of as a form of coercion. This last remark is subject to the restriction mentioned above: if 'coercion' just means that I leave you with no 'reasonable alternative', there might be states of society in which it would be thought unreasonable to turn down an offer which in another context or society would count as a bribe.

Both Russell and Weber analyse power as a property of the intentional action of a human individual. During the past two decades, though, under the influence of Foucault, many theorists have attempted to move in the direction of a more structural and less strictly intentional understanding of phenomena like 'power' (and coercion). In his discussion of the history of penal systems, Foucault discusses Bentham's project of a 'panopticon'.[14] The 'panopticon' was a way of arranging the space in a

---

[14] M. Foucault, *Surveiller et punir* (Paris: Gallimard, 1975), esp. pp. 196–229. See also his 'Le nuage et la poussière', in *L'impossible prison* (Paris: Seuil, 1980), and 'Power and Knowledge', in *Power/Knowledge*, ed. C. Gordon (London: Harvester: 1976).

prison so that the prisoners felt that they were under constant surveillance, even if they were not. Foucault's point is that in such a prison the
prisoners are clearly subject to a very distinct coercive 'power', but this
'power' is not obviously best analysed as a property of the intentional
action of any human individual or group of individuals. It is, as it were,
the space of the prison itself which is powerful and coercive.

To be sure, the prisoners would not be subject to this power, if they
had not been condemned by a jury, sentenced by a judge, assigned to
this prison rather than another by an administrator. The immediate,
everyday face of penal power will be a group of guards, officers, and
a warden. However, these wardens and guards operate according to
regulations and to the possibilities inherent in the institutions, buildings,
etc., in which they find themselves. If one goes back far enough many
other individuals and their intentions will appear in the genealogical
account: the legislators who defined the crimes for which incarceration
is set as the penalty, the persons who commissioned, those who designed,
and those who actually built the physical structure of the prison, and so
on. These agents, too, will have had intentions in acting, although their
intentions may have been highly various. In addition, these intentions
will have had little to do with the actual mode of operation of the power
which emerges partly as a result of the actions these agents performed.
The prison building may have originally been constructed as a fortress
by persons who had no idea that centuries later it would serve as a place
of incarceration, and many members of the jury may have had only
the very vaguest notion of what it was the condemned person would be
subjected to. The better one understands the prison system, the wider
one casts the net in the present and past, the more the very idea of power
as related to what any individual wants or intends gets lost.

Foucault is not concerned, as Weber, I think, was, to distinguish sharply
between power (strictly so-called) and such things as influence.[15] The
Foucauldian programme of construing modern society as the locus of
a dense network of 'omnipresent, but not omnipotent power'[16] seems
to be a significantly more flexible and realistic way of approaching the
phenomenon of power than that centred on the intentional action of

---

[15] Foucault holds that wherever there is power there is the possibility of resistance. See his *L'histoire
de la sexualité: La volonté de savoir* (Paris: Seuil, 1976), pp. 121 ff. I assume that this means that
wherever there is the specific kind of *social* power in which political thinkers have been mainly
interested, there is the possibility of resistance. I suspect that the reason Foucault holds this view
is that he is primarily interested in what he calls the 'disciplinary' form of social power and such
forms require a certain amount of minimal co-operation in order to be acquired or exercised.

[16] 'Le nuage et la poussière', pp. 34f.

individual agents. Individual human beings in such a scheme have power to the extent to which they have socially located and conditioned abilities to do things.

3. THE CONCEPT OF THE STATE

States for Weber are political associations which satisfy two further conditions. First of all, the rules that constitute the order of the 'state' are *imposed* on all the members of some designated group of people, for instance on all those who find themselves in a certain geographic area, or on all those who are the biological descendants of a certain group of people, whether the people in question wish or agree to be subject to those rules or not. Adherence to the rules of the state is not, that is, voluntary, although a 'political association' in Weber's sense could in principle have been completely voluntary.

The claim that an association is completely voluntary is ambiguous as between at least two quite distinct things.[17] An association can be voluntary in that it can be fully up to me whether or not I join, that is, my entrance into the association can depend on my free decision. Second, it can be up to me to leave the association at any time, so when and under what conditions I exit from the association can be a matter of my choice alone. Obviously, too, an association can have involuntary entrance, but be voluntary as far as exit is concerned, or vice versa.

The contrast in this respect between a political association and a state can be brought out by imagining, for instance, a situation in which the basic institutions of the British state had all broken down and we had returned to a condition of near anarchy. Under such circumstances I and some particular individual others, for instance, a large group of people who live in the hovels that once were the City of Cambridge, could have come together, voluntarily agreed on a set of rules to govern our interaction (taken over, perhaps, from an old European Union handbook which had survived), and named some Overseers with power to coerce us to follow the rules we had agreed on. We might also have allowed free exit

---

[17] Obviously whether or not the entrance into or exit from an association is voluntary is a distinct question from the question whether the association is in the fullest sense 'free'. A free association in the fullest sense would be one in which it was not only the case that entry and exit were voluntary, but also one which was characterised by a third important feature, namely that the members of the association had some kind of control over the nature of their interaction (i.e. over the rules that constitute the association) while they were members of the association. I will discuss some of these issues further in chapter 2 §3. See also A. Hirschmann, *Exit, Voice, and Loyalty* (Cambridge, Mass.: Harvard University Press, 1970).

(although if conditions 'outside' were sufficiently grim we might hesitate to speak of fully free exit). Anyone who had not thus voluntarily – or at any rate, explicitly – entered the 'Cambridge Political Association', as we might style ourselves, and who did not voluntarily remain in the association would not be subject to the rules and thus not subject to the authority of the Overseers. We might simply be uninterested in foreigners, casual visitors from the next shire, locals who did not wish to join, or even defectors from our Association – those who had not joined our association or who had left – and not make any attempt to impose our rules on them.

A state, however, is not like that. People who find themselves in France will be subject to the coercive authority of the French state whether they wish it or not. In France I will be forced to post public notices for my business in French whether I am a citizen or not, and even if most of my clientele speaks Arabic: I will be forced to use French postage stamps on my letters, even if I think British stamps are aesthetically more pleasing. I can exit from this jurisdiction only by physically leaving the territory of the state.[18] This is a fundamental fact about states and one of the reasons why attempts to legitimise the state by reference to the consent of the members – for instance, social contract theories – have an uphill battle from the very start, and do not have much prospect of final success. States are not and are not intended to be voluntary associations. It is a great merit of Weber's account that he is not obsessed with trying to square the circle by presenting as 'voluntary' something which is self-evidently deeply non-voluntary. This allows him to avoid the radical bad faith of most social contract theories.

In describing the 'Cambridge Political Association' I was careful to ask the reader to imagine a situation in which there was no 'state' in the full sense of the word, and this was important in getting the example going. It is part of our common understanding of the state (one which Weber shares), that if a state exists, it is unlikely to tolerate practices like the setting up of the Cambridge Political Association. This claim to monopoly is a deeper fact about the state than its involuntariness, and it is what makes the state non-voluntary. An association can, of course, be involuntary without being one in which any agency attempts to monopolise the use of force, but one that tries to monopolise the use of violence – at any rate within a fixed geographic territory – will be very

---

[18] I take the 'geographic' reading, but a parallel case can be made for non-geographically defined associations with imposed rules. In certain versions of Christianity, baptism or entry into certain religious orders may be construed as decisions that, once voluntarily made, subject one to an authority that cannot be revoked.

likely to be non-voluntary, if only because it will not allow voluntary exit from the association. Those who break the rules that govern the use of force within a fixed area cannot be permitted simply to announce their exit *ad libitum*, if the Overseers are to maintain a monopoly on the use of force in any real sense.

The second condition, then, which a political association must satisfy in order to be counted as a 'state' in Weber's sense is that it must successfully monopolise the legitimate exercise of violence.[19] A political association in Weber's sense, as we have seen, has a mechanism for using force to maintain its rules, but those rules may be very limited and encompass only a very small sphere of possible human actions. A state is a political association whose set of rules (and thus also whose order) is so extensive that *no* use of violence is excluded from regulation, and only violence authorised by the association is deemed to be legitimate.[20]

To put it another way, for a political association to exist there must (definitionally, for Weber) be *one* specially designated class of violent actions – those of the potential enforcement of the rules of the association. Such a class of actions must exist, although it is an open question how much force may be used and under what specific circumstances, or, for that matter, whether force ever is *actually* used. In addition, the Overseers must actually succeed (through whatever means, including *perhaps* force) in maintaining the existing order of the association, that is, in preventing it from being dissolved by non-observance of the rules. Apart from this, nothing is said either about how the members of the association are to think about the moral standing of the force used by the Overseers, or about what warrant the Overseers might be thought to have to use force (if necessary). Furthermore, nothing is said in the definition about any *other* acts of coercion or violence that may exist in the society. Whether they will be at all regulated by the rules of the association, and, if so, in what way, is something the definition leaves open. For a state, as opposed to a mere political association, to exist there are *two* designated classes of violent actions. The first class encompasses actions specifically authorised by the association and designated as 'legitimate'. These will include but may not be limited to action undertaken by the Overseers to

---

[19] Weber, 'Politik als Beruf', p. 506.

[20] One of the more striking features of Weber's view is his attempt to give an account of a 'political association' *without* any reference to 'legitimacy' (See *Wirtschaft und Gesellschaft*, p. 16). Thus, when Weber speaks of politics as action relative to 'a political association or state', the 'or' in this statement must be scrutinised carefully. If politics is something that happens in *states* then there will always be a framework of legitimacy-claims in place; this will not necessarily be the case if one approaches politics through the notion of a 'political association'.

enforce the rules. Thus the association may authorise parents to chastise their children, thereby rendering this action 'legitimate'.[21] The second class includes all other acts of violence that might take place within the association; these are designated as 'illegitimate'.

4. THE CONCEPT OF LEGITIMACY

The concept of 'legitimacy' is of such obvious importance for any political philosophy that aspires to be connected with contemporary ways of thinking about the social world that it is worth discussing it at slightly greater length.

'Legitimacy' is a term that occurs in a number of different, although obviously not completely unrelated, contexts that have a direct bearing on politics. First there is 'legitimacy' as a term in international law. A political entity (or organisation or association) is 'legitimate' if it is recognised and accepted by the other established international entities as having the standing of a possible partner for specified kinds of transactions. The question of 'legitimacy' can arise about a number of different entities. Thus one can ask about the legitimacy of a particular organisation or corporation that makes certain claims for itself. 'Is airline X a legitimate international carrier?' means 'has its conformity with various standards been recognised by IATA and the appropriate other international bodies?' 'Is the Romanian Psychoanalytic Association a legitimate training institution?' means 'will its certificates of qualification be recognised as sufficient to allow one to practise psychoanalysis in a variety of countries?' Usually (at least in cases that will interest us), 'legitimate' means 'recognised as a sovereign state' and thus capable of entering into specific relations with other sovereign states on conditions of formal equality. Thus Croatia attains legitimacy in this sense when enough other (recognised) states are willing to sign certain kinds of treaties and conventions with it, exchange ambassadors with it, and so on.

In addition to the question of the legitimacy of a certain entity, one can ask about the legitimacy of a certain specific government or regime or of the personnel who claim to be the representatives of an organisation. Thus the current red–green coalition in Germany led by Gerhard Schröder and Joschko Fischer is legitimate because the representatives named by this government are accepted as the representatives of the Federal Republic of Germany, occupy its seat in the United Nations,

---

[21] *Wirtschaft und Gesellschaft*, p. 30.

NATO, the European Union (EU), etc. In this sense it is a legal and sociological fact like any other fact that the Federal Republic of Germany is 'legitimate' and the Schröder/Fischer administration is its legitimate government. One can support these claims by producing relevant international documents and observing the behaviour of relevant parties, such as diplomats and others.

Although it is a fact that X has the status of being legitimate (being recognised as a subject for various purposes), the ascription of this status is usually not arbitrary – no one has yet invited the trustees of the Whitney Gallery, the Dairy Farmers' Association, the Greater Berlin Mycological Society, or me to become a member of the United Nations (UN) Security Council (together with China, the United Kingdom, etc.).[22] Those who perform these acts of recognition generally claim to be acting on the basis of an evaluation of the extent to which the entity in question satisfies certain criteria. Three are most often mentioned. First, the agency that is a candidate for recognition as a legitimate state actually has effective control over a given territory which it claims. This means that it in fact effectively monopolises the use of force within that area: any force that is used is used by the agencies of the candidate state, or delegates and surrogates which it authorises. This condition is often glossed as equivalent to the claim that the candidate-state actually succeeds in getting its commands obeyed.[23] That this condition is satisfied is a matter that leaves room for a certain amount of interpretation. No really existing social agency, after all, ever *fully* monopolises the use of force, because crime exists even in the most efficient and repressive regime. The continued existence of some violence is, then, no obstacle to legitimacy, but how much is too much? Still, that this condition is satisfied is in principle an empirical matter, provided one takes a moderately generous view of what can count as 'empirical' in the study of human societies.

The second condition is one that tries to take account of how the people who are subject to the power of the candidate-agency in question see their situation and that agency. The agency satisfies this second condition if those subject to its power do not merely conform to its demands and injunctions in the way in which one bows to threats of overwhelming

---

[22] This performative aspect of attributions of legitimacy is well brought out in R. M. Hare's 'The Lawful Government' (in *Philosophy, Politics, and Society, Third Series*, ed. P. Laslett and W. G. Runciman, Oxford: Blackwell, 1967), but the essay could easily give the (incorrect) impression that such attributions are relatively arbitrary.

[23] The fact that these two conditions: 'X effectively monopolises violence' and 'X gets its commands obeyed' are held to be equivalent is a striking phenomenon that would, I think, repay further thought and discussion of a kind I am not in a position to give here.

force. Rather the subjects in question give those injunctions at least some minimal moral standing or take them to have some rudimentary normative force *because* they have been issued by that agency. In the real world of politics one can slip into potentially confusing situations in which a kind of circularity arises: the EU recognises Bosnia and its government (in part) because EU officials think most Bosnians accept that the directives of this government have some normative standing, but the fact that the EU recognises the government may give the Bosnians themselves further reason to take what it commands seriously. It is not clear that there is anything wrong with this kind of circularity. Bosnians may think that whether or not a given regime which claims authority over them is recognised by the EU as legitimate is of great practical importance to them, and they may also be sufficiently sophisticated and/or sufficiently fatalistic to think that recognition by the EU is highly relevant to deciding what practical attitude they should themselves take towards that regime. They may quite reasonably take the fact that the EU recognises the government as a sign that it would not only be prudent to conform to its commands, but that they ought to give its commands some independent normative weight. Still, international recognition is unlikely to be the *only* factor Bosnians will weigh up in trying to decide what to think of a regime to which they are subjected, and in principle it may not be a factor at all.

This second condition is also an empirical one, in a broad sense, although it depends on making a judgement not just about how a group of people acts, but also about how they think they ought to act, and why they think they ought to act in that way. The third condition is that those who perform the act of recognition (e.g. officials at the UN) would also judge that the agency has acquired and is wielding power in the way they (i.e. the officials at the UN) think it ought, and thus that the people who are subject to it are right to think that they ought to obey it. People differ in their moral and political views, and those who are in a position to recognise or withhold recognition may well not have the same views about how power ought to be used and how people ought to act as those who are subject to the candidate-regime do. If they are sufficiently reflective, the agencies who can grant recognition may realise that this is the case, and try to take account of it. There is unlikely to be a formula that will tell us what 'take account of' should mean concretely. It is also, of course, possible to agree with members of group G that they ought to do what a certain regime enjoins and yet disagree on the reasons or grounds on which one thinks that this is a good idea.

So the EU recognises Croatia as legitimate when it believes that the government with its seat in Zagreb actually is able to control violence within a designated area, when the EU judges that (most) people in Croatia think they ought to do what the government in Zagreb commands, and when the relevant agencies in Strasburg and Brussels agree with the opinion they attribute to those in Croatia that people in Croatia ought to do as the government in Zagreb says. As we have seen, in this concrete case the tail wagged the dog because satisfaction of the second and third condition was deemed sufficient even in the absence of effective control over some parts of the national territory. There are, of course, other factors apart from the three I cited that might affect a decision to recognise a state as legitimate. One obvious such factor is the existence of historically existing boundaries, or historical continuity with previously existing regimes or states, or cultural factors. Another might be considerations of economic viability. Obviously the effect of recognition or non-recognition on power-politics is likely to be of crucial importance, but also equally unlikely to be explicitly cited as reason for a decision to recognise or not to recognise.

The use of the word 'legitimate' ('lawful') to designate a corporation or other entity which is recognised in the way outlined above strongly suggests that the entity is recognised *because* it satisfies antecedent rules or standards. Strictly speaking, this is no more true in the case of 'legitimate' than it is in the case of other performatives. In principle the UN could give a seat on the Security Council to anyone, whether or not they satisfied the above three conditions. In fact it was originally argued that Croatia could not be recognised as a legitimate state because it did not control all of the national territory which it claimed, a large portion of that being occupied by Serbian forces. Croatia was eventually recognised despite this fact. In principle a band of terrorists might put themselves in a sufficiently dangerous strategic position for it to be prudent to treat with them as the 'legitimate' government of a particular area, even though virtually no one in the international agencies in question thought they had acquired or were wielding power in an acceptable way, or thought that those subject to the power of the terrorists believed that their directives had the slightest normative standing. It might be so unwise as to constitute an act of preternatural folly to recognise such a group, and give them a seat on the Security Council, but there is nothing about 'legitimacy' (in this sense) which makes such a thing impossible or incoherent.

In addition to this use in international relations, the term 'legitimacy' is also used in a second context. The first context was one in which we had states and established international agencies confronting a candidate-corporation with whom they must decide to deal or not (in one way or another). This second use refers to a situation in which people who are located within an established political association are confronted with certain decisions, commands, directives, or enactments, and a question arises about the standing of such decisions. One can see the connection of this sense of 'legitimate' with the second of the two conditions on which people purportedly base their judgement that a regime is 'legitimate' in the sense of international law.

To ask whether a given decision is 'legitimate' seems to be to ask a two-pronged question. The etymology of the word 'legitimate' (from Latin: *lex*) suggests that the question is one about the relation of the decision to some 'law', or rule, or principle, and so the first prong of this question is: 'Does the decision conform to the laws or principles, or does it follow in the accepted way from the rules?' This first version of the question responds to the surface intention of the query about the legitimacy of a certain command or decision, and in some contexts answering in this way might be fully adequate to satisfy the person who asked the question, for example, if the question was posed in an examination on legal procedures. Nevertheless, the real intention in asking the general question about legitimacy is not to discover whether some enactment has certain formal or procedural properties, but to determine whether that enactment has normative standing for me, and, if so, in what way. One can reasonably try to answer a question about legitimacy by citing conformity to accepted rules because one often simply assumes that if the directive does conform to certain principles or rules it will be binding on me. This assumption is, of course, not always warranted. Perhaps the formal legal system to which the directive conforms is itself deeply flawed or morally reprehensible. The second prong of the question about the legitimacy of a decision, command, or directive is then: 'Should or must I take account of the command in my action, and, if so, in what way?'

The phrase 'according to the rules' in discussions of legitimacy, unless further specified, can mean in the first instance nothing more than 'according to the usual, recognised, prevailing ways of doing things', and this may be extended to include even unwritten rules and traditional ways of proceeding.[24] The question of whether a decision is legitimate

---

[24] This is an instance of a productive kind of anachronism. 'Legitimate' comes into use as a term only when there are 'laws' that are in some sense codified, even if not in writing, to judge actions and decisions. Once one *has* this concept, then, one can apply it retrospectively.

in the sense of being conformable to the (perhaps vague and unwritten) rules and the question whether it is binding are two distinct questions, although certain traditional ways of thinking in philosophy have perhaps tended to collapse the two. It is, however, equally important to keep in mind that even if a decision, order, or enactment is acknowledged as binding on someone, it is a further open question in what *way* it is binding.

Up to now I have spoken of 'normative standing, moral force, binding power, what one ought to take account of, what one ought to obey' in a relatively uncontrolled way, and as if these were all clearly defined terms that were also all more or less interchangeable. There are, however, a number of very different ways in which purportedly legitimate directives might been seen to bear on my action. Even if we take what might seem to be the clearest and narrowest of the concepts, that of having binding power, this can mean a number of different things.

To say that something is binding is to say that there is a sanction associated with violating it. Thus a law is legally binding if there are legal penalties associated with transgressing it. A principle is morally binding if violation of it warrants moral condemnation. The dictates of reason may be binding in that I show myself to be a fool if I fail to observe them. I may give you very good grounds for thinking I am rash if I ignore counsels of prudence, and in that sense they may be said to have (some) binding power. In some of these cases the 'sanction' is ethereal in the extreme, but it is still important to distinguish between sanctions of different kinds (a prison sentence, or showing oneself to be a rash person) and strengths, and it seems senseless to speak of binding power with reference to some sanction. To consider an example, in a medical case I may summon one specialist after another. The opinion of a specialist may have more standing than my neighbour's off-hand observations about how I look today, but the opinion of any one specialist may not be definitive; we know that physicians sometimes disagree. After numerous conferences, however, a large number of specialists may all come to agree on a diagnosis and recommended treatment, and this may well represent the best that prevailing medical science has to offer. If I ignore this advice I may show myself to be a fool, but I will not necessarily have shown myself to be immoral.

Similarly, there might exist such things as an institution of a board of arbitration which is set up to deal with disputes of a certain kind. We might now ask whether a certain ruling made by this board was legitimate, meaning whether the board was constituted in accordance with the customary rules governing such things and whether it proceeded in the proper way to give judgement. Even if these conditions were satisfied it might still be the case, though, that the judgement given was merely advisory or hortatory, and that compliance with the finding of the board was voluntary. It might be unreasonable, or unfair, or immoral for me to ignore the decision, but that decision, even if it is reached in a way that follows all the rules, might also not be legally binding. Even if the decision *is* 'binding' in the sense that it gives a definitive judgement that I would be extremely unwise to fail to take into account, it does not follow from that that I am *obligated to obey* it.

I give these examples in particular to press home the point not just that there are a variety of different ways and different degrees to which something can have normative force for me, but to counter a certain insinuation that one sometimes finds. It is sometimes suggested that there is a simple and exhaustive dichotomy here between some judgement or decision having no standing for me whatever, and it having the standing of being absolutely and categorically binding, so that it must be obeyed at all costs and under any circumstances. So far from this being the case, there is much room between these two extremes, and it is in this space that most of politics is located.

A particular directive, demand, or injunction is usually issued by some agent or agency: the Board of Arbitration says that Richard (not Joan) should get the disputed cow; the assembled doctors recommend chemotherapy; the Chamber of Deputies resolves that action X shall be taken. Once one has begun asking about the legitimacy of any given single, specific directive with special reference to its normative standing for me, and has received the answer that it has standing because it was issued by some person or agency according to rules, it is natural to go on to ask why that person or agency can give me a directive (admittedly according to rules) which I must take seriously. This is the question of the legitimacy of the agency. We are inclined to phrase this question as: does it have 'authority' (and if so, what kind)?

5. AUTHORITY

'Authority' is used in a number of senses, but all of the various uses of the term can be seen as grouped around a central core usage. I will claim that this central case is one in which we speak of a person (A) who takes another person (B) to have authority, or to be an authority, with respect to some domain or area (Δ). A takes B to be an authority on Δ or to have authority with respect to Δ, if A believes he or she has reason to take what B says with respect to Δ seriously, simply because it is B who says it, and irrespective of any independent judgement A may make about Δ. The various senses in which 'authority' is used can all be fitted into this schema.[25]

The first of the senses in which 'authority' is used is epistemic authority. This is the property I have by virtue of possessing theoretical knowledge, being a reliable source of information, or a skilful practitioner of a certain craft. Thus if I am 'an authority' on the poetry of Catullus or the functioning of the human liver, and you take me to be such an authority, then you think that you are well advised to rely on what I say about the metrics of Catullus' poems, or about the long-term effects of excessive consumption of alcohol. You also think that you are well advised to do this independently of any antecedent views you might have about Catullus or the human liver. My view on these subjects carries weight with you simply because it is my view, because it is I who hold and propound it. To say I am an authority on Catullus, or that you take me to be an authority on Catullus, in no way implies that I have a warrant to give you orders, or that I can expect to be obeyed if I give orders (e.g. about the punctuation of a particular Catullan text or about what diet one should follow in order to maximise one's chances of having a healthy liver). As a general principle it is not even necessarily 'foolish' to ignore the assertions of someone with epistemic authority. Decisions on how to punctuate a text might perfectly reasonably be governed *not* exclusively by the directive of those with authority about Catullus, but by persons who are sensitive to aesthetic, political, or commercial considerations. Having a healthy liver may not under all circumstances be the *non plus ultra* of human life.[26]

Philosophers have repeatedly been tempted to construe all forms of 'authority' on the model of epistemic authority. There is a conservative and authoritarian variant of this strategy, which one can find in Plato[27] and Gadamer,[28] which attempts this assimilation in order to cast a glow of superior knowledge and wisdom around existing relations of political

---

[25] See the excellent discussion of authority in J. Raz, *The Morality of Freedom* (Oxford: Oxford University Press, 1986), chapters 2–4.

[26] Plato puts this point forcefully in various early dialogues, e.g. *Gorgias*, 511a–513c.

[27] Plato, *Republic*, *passim*.

[28] G. Gadamer, *Wahrheit und Methode* (Tübingen: Mohr, 1960), esp. pp. 250–90, and also his essays in *Die Vernunft im Zeitalter der Wissenschaft* (Frankfurt/M: Suhrkamp, 1980). A similar position is defended by P. Winch in his 'Authority', in *Political Philosophy*, ed. A. Quinton (Oxford: Oxford University Press, 1967).

authority, and a liberal variant (as in Raz)[29] which uses the analogy with epistemic authority to argue that political authority should be conceived to be limited in scope and essentially advisory.

Nevertheless, on our usual conception at any rate, political authority seems to differ significantly from epistemic authority. A person who holds political authority is not just in possession of knowledge which it would be unwise to ignore (if one needed information about the subject in question), but has a warrant to command of some kind and should be able to expect to be obeyed. The papyrologist may or may not be able to say definitively and 'authoritatively' that a certain scrap is from second-century Egypt, but nothing much follows from this for my action, unless I happen to be a historian who is about to publish a conjecture that depends on a particular dating of this particular scrap. It may, then, be unwise for me to ignore the papyrologist's view, but that will depend very much on my own purposes and it is not in any sense immoral, nor can the papyrologist in any way coerce obedience. Epistemic authority seems concerned in the first instance with declarative propositions: 'This papyrus fragment is from second century Egypt', 'Her liver will not be able to tolerate that amount of regular consumption of alcohol in the long run'; '"*Glubit*" in this poem probably means . . . ' Political authority, on the other hand, seems characteristically concerned with commands and prohibitions.

The second possible sense in which 'authority' is used is to designate what is sometimes called 'natural authority'.[30] The usual examples which are given to illustrate this include that of a ship in distress. There may be someone on board who *de facto*, by virtue of some quirk of personality, is capable of mobilising to a high degree the instinct for conformity and emulation that is part of the psychic make-up of most people and of getting them to follow directives.[31] We usually think of compliance under such circumstances as being voluntary, or at any rate not the result of external coercion or fear of punishment, although it is perhaps also true that response to such natural authority is keener and stronger in situations of clear external danger. I do what the person in question says because there is something about him or her that positively and attractively impresses and reassures me. Such a person may hold no formal position or office, and thus has no warrant. In fact, the people

---

[29] Raz, *Morality of Freedom.*

[30] See R. Peters, 'Authority', in *Political Philosophy*, ed. A. Quinton (Oxford: Oxford University Press, 1967).

[31] This is what Max Weber calls 'charismatic authority'. See *Wirtschaft und Gesellschaft*, pp. 124–58.

on a foundering ship who *do* hold the formal warrants to give orders – the captain and officers – may be incapable of getting themselves obeyed, may lack this 'natural authority', and this deficiency may render null the fact that they have the formal warrants. This kind of authority may be very like epistemic authority, at least if one construes epistemic authority sufficiently broadly to include mastery of skills in addition to possession of propositional knowledge. The reason I obey a certain person on the ship without asking questions or trying to form my own opinion about what should be done may be that this person seems to be an expert in organising people or in getting things done efficiently. On the other hand 'natural authority' is an interesting phenomenon precisely because I may not be able to say exactly why I think I have reason to take seriously what a person with natural authority says.

A third sense of authority is the *de facto* political authority described above on p. 32: certain people actually control a certain area; they monopolise the use of violence and succeed in getting their commands obeyed. The fact that a well-established political regime or occupation forces have overwhelming strength and use it ruthlessly may give me good reason to do what they tell me, at any rate in certain areas of life. Sometimes *de facto* is used expansively to include both this sense and 'natural authority', but when the two are being distinguished, people usually mean to emphasise that '*de facto* political authority' may contain a strong element of compulsion or the threat of use of physical force, whereas this is thought to be absent when we speak of natural authority.

In the fourth sense certain people may have what is called '*de jure* authority': that is, there is a law that prescribes that people should obey them. Thus the captain of the foundering ship has *de jure* authority in that he has a warrant to command: the company statutes and the international laws of the sea prescribe that he is to be obeyed (within certain limits). He may have this *de jure* authority while lacking all natural authority and lacking *de facto* authority: in the case in question no one pays any attention at all to his confused commands.

Many philosophers, however, have not been satisfied with distinguishing merely these four senses of authority, and have thought that something important is still left out. That the captain of a ship is able to get his orders obeyed is just a fact (or not, as the case may be); that he has a warrant in the sense in which this has been discussed up to now is also just a fact (perhaps a 'sociological' fact). Perhaps we can trace the authority of this warrant back through a series of steps: first to the shipping company, then to some kind of national board of maritime affairs, then to international regulatory agencies and courts and eventually to the immemorial, customary law of the sea, and its pedigree may be impeccable all the way back until it peters out into obscure indeterminacy. Some philosophers have argued that the existence of such a warrant may itself be no more than a further sociological fact with no real normative standing. We know that it sometimes happens that warrants are formally fully in order and sociologically completely unquestioned in a given society yet we feel free to reject them. Thus in some ancient societies there were licensed slave-catchers. These men did not simply *de facto* get away with catching and selling slaves; they may well have had warrants that satisfied all the then existing rules, derived from the best existing authorities, and were accepted without question by all the then existing legal and political institutions. Still we may deny that they had '*de jure* authority' to catch people as slaves (in one sense of '*de jure* authority') because *we* think that there ought not to be such an authority or such a warrant. That is, we recognise that the existing moral, legal, and political institutions agree in granting this warrant. The slave-catchers in that sense have '*de jure* authority' – authority derived from law – but we think that this is a sign that the whole political and social system is, in this particular feature at least, normatively defective. This is a fifth sense of 'authority'.

In this fifth sense it is not sufficient for X to have a warrant that is legally correct or conforms to *some* set of rules (including the most highly regarded contemporary rules). X has 'authority' in this sense only if X has a warrant which will stand up to some further moral scrutiny that could be brought to bear on it and on the whole system of accepted rules from which it derives. That is, X has '*de jure* authority' in this fifth sense if X has a warrant that 'ought to' be obeyed, where the 'ought' is relative to some more or less free-standing moral judgement we make. I will sometimes call this '*de jure* authority in the philosophical or fully normative sense', and contrast it with '*de jure* authority' in the fourth sense analysed above, which we might call the 'descriptive' or 'sociological' sense.

In cases like that of the licensed slave-catchers *we* may be tempted to say that '*de facto*' they had the authority to do this, but not '*de jure*' (i.e. they ought not to have been permitted to do this). This indicates a potential confusion which arises from the attempt to force what is in fact a tripartite distinction into a binary form (*de facto/de jure*). The tripartite distinction is between: (a) purely *de facto* authority – that of a person who effectively has control, regardless of whether that person has any warrant at all (i.e. the third sense above), (b) *de jure* authority (i.e. the fourth, the 'sociological' sense above) – that of a person who has a warrant that is socio-culturally 'in order' ('legally valid', given the existing laws) regardless of whether that person can actually succeed in being obeyed and regardless also of what *we* may think about whether the warrant ought to carry weight, whether the 'law' from which it is derived ought to hold, and (c) '*de jure* authority' (in the full normative sense) – that of a person who has a warrant that will stand up to whatever normative scrutiny we wish to subject such things to (the fifth sense above). Sense (b) is *de jure* relative to sense (a), but we are tempted to say that it is 'merely' *de facto* relative to (c).[32]

We may use senses (b) and (c) above to make a parallel set of distinctions about the concept of legitimacy. A decision or a regime might fail to be legitimate (in a descriptively *de jure* sense, parallel to (b) in the previous paragraph) because it failed to conform to accepted rules properly. It is, however, also in principle always possible for us to make independent moral judgements about the 'accepted rules', and so we can also judge a decision or regime 'legitimate' or not (in a normatively '*de jure*' sense, parallel to (c) above) if it survives or fails to survive scrutiny by our preferred criteria of moral judgement.

With that we can return to Max Weber's definition of the state which we left at the end of the last section, and see that the 'legitimacy' which is an essential component of a state for him is descriptively *de jure* legitimacy. A state is not *only* a form of direct constant coercion, but it is also a structure that is embedded in and may to some extent secrete around itself some moral and legal apparatus of beliefs and rules about what is and is not warranted, and in particular takes it upon itself to define certain actions as 'legitimate' and others as 'illegitimate' (not just as actions that it will tolerate and actions that it will repress). Without this, there is no *state* but merely a condition of more or less organised raiding. On the other hand, the sense of 'legitimate' will not necessarily be one that will stand up to any very sophisticated form of independent moral reflection or scrutiny, so a state need not necessarily be legitimate in the fully normative *de jure* sense.

6. WEBER'S 'MODERN' STATE

As I have said, Weber's *general* account of the state is sociological and functional: the state is understood as whatever successfully monopolises

---

[32] A topic of understandable importance which political philosophers have frequently discussed is the relation between authority and power. This discussion will be utterly confused unless one begins by trying to be clear first which of the five kinds of authority one has in mind and second whether one means by 'power' just (reliable) ability to get something done or ability to get one's own will despite opposition.

the legitimate use of force without anything being said about how this monopolisation takes place, how it is institutionalised, and so on. To give a functional account of the kind Weber proposes is precisely *not* to give a teleological account, which attributes to an entity an inherent goal, purpose, or aim. Thus, it is often claimed, in the ancient world various philosophers thought that the πόλις had the inherent goal of allowing humans to live the best life possible for them, and Hegel distinguished pretty clearly between the functions a state had to discharge – keeping the economy running by deft intervention – from the inherent and defining goal of the state: 'allowing the members to lead a universal life'.[33]

One obvious difference between Weber's functional analysis and the teleological approaches that are perhaps more characteristic of a certain kind of philosopher is that Weber's starts from observation of successful functioning. A state exists when legitimate use of coercion is successfully monopolised in the society; otherwise no state exists. Success is not built into the teleological approach: an entity may be inherently oriented towards the attainment of some goal and yet fail to reach that goal. As Hegel says,[34] a sick or demented human being who may be incapable of leading a universal life is still a human being; a neutered tom-cat who is incapable of attaining his inherent goal of reproducing his species is still a cat.

A second difference between functional and teleological views is that a sociologist like Weber is radically disillusioned; the description of the successful functioning of the state is a view from *outside*, which does not automatically invite moralising. The state is merely an agency operating and exercising powers in a certain way. Part of the object being observed, to be sure, is a set of beliefs about legitimacy held by the members of the state under consideration, but the sociologist may or may not be interested in assessing these beliefs morally. The teleological view, on the other hand, is one from the inside, that is, one that virtually cries out for us to make a commitment to or take a position on the designated goal and the state as a way to strive to attain that goal. The teleological view is morally insinuating. The position we take may be positive (we endorse the state and identify with its values) or negative (as philosophical anarchists we may reject the state and all its works), but it requires a great effort of the imagination to remain neutral in the face of *this* kind of analysis.

As Weber continues his discussion, however, he begins to add structural conditions to his notion of the state. Thus, for instance, immediately

---

[33] G. W. F Hegel, *Grundlinien der Philosophie des Rechts*, in *Werke in zwanzig Bänden*, ed. E. Moldenhauer and K. M. Michel (Frankfurt/M: Suhrkamp, 1970), vol. VII, §258.

[34] Ibid. vol. VII, §258Z.

after defining the state he distinguishes a specifically 'modern' form of the state from other forms. The distinction is made along three dimensions, at least two of which refer not to particular distinct functions but to specific structural features of the societies in question. First, a modern state is characterised by a particular tripartite internal structure which pre-modern states lack. Pre-modern societies are either egalitarian, as is the case with many tribal societies, or they exhibit a straightforward bipartite structure of 'haves' and 'have-nots', those who hold power and those who do not, rulers and subjects. In a modern state there are not two but three sociologically substantial, functionally distinct groups: (1) rulers, (political) leaders, (2) functionaries, administrative officers, bureaucrats, civil servants, etc., and (3) the mass of the population, the 'ruled'.[35] In principle the distinction between (1), (2), and (3) is between those who make the decisions, those who carry out the decisions, and those who are subject to the power of those who make and carry out the decisions. It is the lack of this middle group of functionaries in many ancient and medieval political associations which makes them very different from modern states.[36] Thus, in fifth-century Athens virtually all administrative functions were discharged by ordinary citizens in rotation (with the help of a certain number of public slaves who were not citizens at all). Second, it is essential for the existence of a modern state that the rulers, and also the functionaries, the members of the administrative staff, do not own or have effective private control over the resources and instruments used in administration. Thus in some pre-modern Western societies certain important public functions were exercised by feudal dignitaries. When the King went to war he summoned his barons who appeared with *their* troops. The barons may have had some independent political authority of their own, and will often have owned (in an effective legal sense) much of the military equipment used, such as horses, weapons, carts. A baron could hold court and try legal cases in a building he himself owned, in what we might call his 'private' house. In the modern world admirals do not own the aircraft-carriers they command, nor

---

[35] One popular theory of democracy is committed to the claim that in such a political system groups 1 and 3 are identical (and in most such theories there is no place for a distinct group like 2). Weber's account is in the first instance intended as a sociological description of the facts in modern states. The democratic theory is intended as a moral view. There is an important question whether that moral view is compatible with the social reality Weber describes (assuming he has described it more or less correctly).

[36] A standard older treatment of feudal societies is M. Bloch, *Feudal Society* (Chicago: University of Chicago Press, 1961, 2 vols.). One can find a good description of the workings of Athenian democracy in M. Hansen, *The Athenian Democracy in the Age of Demosthenes* (Oxford: Blackwell, 1991).

does a judge own the building in which he or she presides. The military apparatus of a modern army, tanks, helicopters, bases, etc., is not the private property of anyone, neither of those who drive the tanks, nor of those who order them to be driven in one direction rather than another. This apparatus is free-standing and can be activated or directed by anyone holding the proper warrant. This actual split between the 'private' property of individuals and the public apparatus of administration is historically crucial not only in the formation of the modern state as an actually existing entity, but also in the genesis of the very idea of a 'state' as a free-standing, abstract locus of power and (potential) authority.

The modern state is an abstract structure of offices endowed with powers, warrants, and resources which are distinguished sharply from the contingent human occupants of these offices. Thus one can argue abstractly for or against the legitimacy or desirability of this entity. That is, one can argue about whether it is a good idea that there be such a thing as a state, an abstract structure of offices having control over a certain very extensive apparatus of coercion, and one can argue for or against granting this entity certain further powers and resources. All these arguments can be conducted to some extent *independently* of one's views about the actual powers and moral properties of the persons who are the incumbents of the various state-offices at any given time. Equally one can develop an abstract loyalty (or disapproval) of the whole structure, independent of one's judgement about the soundness of general policies it pursues, the wisdom of particular decisions it makes, and the morality of the particular persons who happen to hold office. In speaking of 'the state' or 'the modern state' I have something different in mind from 'the government' or the 'form of government'. The 'form of government' designates the particular relations that hold between specific offices, and 'the government' refers usually to the distinct group of people who occupy those offices. A modern state can remain the same despite a change in government (when Major is defeated and Blair elected) or even in form of government (when France or Italy undergo constitutional reform).

This leads naturally to the third feature Weber claims to observe in specifically modern states, an appeal to a particular kind of legitimacy which he calls legal-rational.[37] In pre-modern forms of society personal

---

[37] Weber distinguishes three kinds of (*de facto*) legitimacy: traditional, charismatic, and rational-legal. This is a distinction relative to the kinds of reasons people have for accepting that a given directive is to be obeyed, either because they have always obeyed directives of that kind (originating from that person or that person's ancestors), because the person has striking personal properties, or because they hold that there is a rule that requires obedience of this kind (p. 124).

attributes and characteristics can provide potential leaders with a kind of *de facto* warrant to command, in that they motivate followers to want to obey; Weber speaks of 'charismatic leadership' in cases like this. In a modern state, however, the abstract and non-personal nature of the structure as a whole means that legitimacy itself must become a matter of abstract reasoning and formal rules. If I am shipwrecked, I may do what Ethel says because I like her, because she radiates what we call 'natural authority', and because she is obviously more competent in things that matter under those circumstances, such as food preparation, than I am – what she cooks tends to be digestible, what I or the other castaways cook I vomit up within half an hour. If, however, Ethel works for the Taxation Authority, and is in addition a merely marginally competent and wholly obnoxious person, I will need a set of more general abstract reasons (referring probably to forms of legislation) to be motivated to think I ought to follow her directives (although, as we will see later, the meaning and force of this 'ought' will be open to question).

Max Weber was not the only one to propose a functional understanding of the state. A second functional approach to the state is that of Marx. For him the state has the function of extracting, storing, and distributing economic surplus. To be sure, in order to discharge this task efficiently, it is necessary to maintain a certain degree of public order. This means that in fact there will virtually always be agencies for exercising coercive force in the societies, because one cannot, for instance, have the granaries broken into *ad libitum*. How these agencies are organised will vary through history, and Marx thinks that if viewed from a sufficient historical distance this variation will finally be seen to depend on the level of technical control of the world and economic productivity. In the conditions of relatively low development of human technological power that have prevailed in the world until relatively recently, Marx thinks, to maintain the economically necessary minimal public order required the existence of a sociologically distinct structure of coercion, that is armed men who are not themselves direct producers but are supported – literally fed – by the direct producers. The maintenance of such order, however, is a distinctly subordinate function and one which the state discharges in order to be able to get on with its main task of economic management. It might not be thought to matter that much if the agricultural workers beat each other up in an unregulated way or kill vagrants or economically marginal or unproductive persons, as long as they continue to draw water, and plough the fields or work in the rice paddies. Maintenance of that order which is necessary for the collection and management of an economic surplus is a much weaker requirement than *monopolisation* of legitimate violence, and in the Marxist scheme control of violence is merely a means which the state uses, not its defining feature.

Marx did not use the language of 'function', of course, which historically had not yet established itself as a major way of thinking about society. Rather he speaks of 'powers'. The state has powers of regulation, but these powers are located in a set of institutions – notably the police, the standing army, and the bureaucracy – which is separate from the rest of society, so that members of the society as a whole precisely do *not* have direct control over them. The police step in to *stop* the enraged inhabitants of the town from lynching the local drug dealer, and for the police to be fully subject to popular control would render it unable to do this. For Marx a state, or, as he often puts it, a 'political state', exists when such powers of economic organisation are located in a separate structure.[38] This is why he says, for example, that the United States was not a state in the nineteenth century (because, presumably, it had no standing army, centralised police force, and so on). The distinction between the powers of the (modern) state and the characteristic institutional structure of such a state is one that is of crucial importance for Marx. The next stage of history, he thinks, is a form of society in which the powers of organisation characteristic of the modern state are retained, but are no longer located in a distinct coercive apparatus; instead they are, as he says, to be 'reabsorbed into society as a whole'. Thus instead of a centralised national police force, local people in each town would supervise traffic, investigate crimes, etc., perhaps using a system of rotation so that no one was stuck with any one task for too long, economic planning would be in the hands of the immediate producers who actually worked in the factories, and so on.

7. HISTORY AND THE CONCEPT OF THE STATE

When – that is, at what historical time – do we begin to find among the agents in the world not just individuals, families, tribes, cities, and feudal regimes of one kind of another, but proper 'states'? Whatever might be the case with genes, tectonic plates, or black holes, a group of armed persons becomes a 'police force' (rather than, say a 'gang') only if it is embedded in a social context in which people have *some* beliefs about

---

[38] K. Marx, '*Zur Judenfrage*', in *Marx-Engels Werke* (Berlin: Dietz Verlag, 1957) vol. 1.

distinctions between formal and informal, controlled and uncontrolled, authorised and unauthorised kinds of violence. It is perhaps not strictly necessary for them to have a single word for the concept 'police', because human languages are very flexible and periphrasis is often easy and efficient. This allows us to attribute to certain past agents rudimentary forms of concepts for which they may have had no distinct term. Routinisation, however, is also a pervasive feature of human life and if appropriately authorised armed gangs become a regular feature of a human society, we can expect that a usual way of referring to them (and distinguishing them from other groups) will eventually establish itself, although the way of referring to them may seem peculiar to us. Thus the word closest to our 'police' in fifth century Attic seems to have been 'the Skythians', designating (originally) the nationality of the state-slaves employed for purposes of maintaining public order.

Similar remarks apply to the 'state'. Because of the basic looseness of historical fit between words, concepts, and social reality, we can expect to encounter a certain unclarity concerning both the proper meaning of terms like 'state' as used by agents in the past and the reality of the social institution it purports to designate. The study of the history of concepts is, however, a particularly fruitful way of gaining initial access to our practically central human institutions.

The word 'state' is, even today, notoriously ambiguous in English between a very general use that has no particular political connotations at all and a sense that purports to pick out a very specific kind of political entity. To speak of 'the state of my house', referring to the accumulated filth of almost a decade that lies strewn around in various parts of the fabric, is to use the term in the first of these senses; 'the state must intervene in the economy to prevent the growth of unemployment' is an illustration of its political use. As Quentin Skinner has shown very convincingly,[39] only very gradually in the late sixteenth and early seventeenth centuries did the word 'state' (and its analogues in most Western European languages) come to acquire a specifically political meaning, as referring to a distinct entity entrusted with exercising civil authority through a separate structure of offices and powers. Before that time there is no single identifiable word that was used to designate the entity which we now usually call 'the state' in the political sense.

The absence in the ancient and medieval worlds of a term that corresponds very closely to our word 'state' is hidden by the fact that translators

[39] Q. Skinner, 'The State', in *Political Innovation and Conceptual Change*, ed. T. Ball, J. Farr, and R. L. Hanson (eds.) (Cambridge: Cambridge University Press, 1989), pp. 89–131.

very often introduce the word 'state' into their translations of older texts to render what are in fact very different notions. Thus the first sentence of Aristotle's *Politics* in the nineteenth-century translation by Jowett (revised by J. Barnes in 1984),[40] reads: 'Every state is a community of some kind . . .' However the Greek word which is here rendered 'state' is πόλις, i.e. a word which is more usually and more correctly translated as 'city'. One can see how this sort of mistake arises. Aristotle's *Politics*, the translator thinks (correctly), deals with the basic issues of politics, and starts with an account of the fundamental framework within which politics takes place. However, the translator reflects, the basic framework within which politics takes place *for us* is the state. This reflection is also arguably correct. To translate, though, is to render what was comprehensible to them, comprehensible to us. Therefore, the translator continues (incorrectly), we should render the term Aristotle uses for the basic framework of politics (πόλις) with the term we use for the basic framework of politics ('state').

Most interesting concepts in politics have a highly flexible extension, and once we have the word and concept 'state' nothing prevents us from extending its use backward beyond what it was originally intended to designate. Doing this, however, makes it difficult, if not impossible, for the study of the history of political thought to make one of the most important contributions it can make to expanding our political understanding. How does the world of politics look if you have no concept of the state?

Only in the late sixteenth and early seventeenth centuries does the state become established as an independent, free-standing entity in three dimensions, first in the dimension of social and historical reality, second conceptually, and third morally. In this period there begin to emerge in Western Europe entities that have some of the structural properties that Max Weber correctly describes as characteristic of the modern state. The general distinction between an office and the person or persons who happen to occupy that office at a certain time – between the consulship and Cicero as a particular incumbent – is a very old one, but the distinction between personal and 'official' powers was often elusive. In some Western European countries at the start of the early modern period, this distinction becomes sharper and hardens as there arises a separate, highly structured domain of offices, and associated with these offices a greatly accumulated set of powers, resources, instruments which were not really under the effective personal control of those who happened

---

[40] This nineteenth-century translation is still the basis of the most widely used recent versions, for instance that edited by S. Everson and published by Cambridge University Press in 1988.

to occupy the offices at any given time. In addition, such societies begin to exhibit the modern tri-partite structure of rulers/functionaries/ruled. Parallel to this, the term 'state' comes into existence in its use to designate this abstractly defined set of offices and associated powers. Finally, in the third dimension 'the state' comes to be seen as an entity which can claim for itself a distinct, overriding, civil authority in its own right. This authority is construed as distinct in two directions. On the one hand, the authority of the state is not *merely* the authority of the people who constitute the subjects of the state, either individually or collectively. In this direction the invention of the concept of the state is part of a strategy for opposing the doctrine of popular sovereignty. On the other hand, the authority of the state is distinct from the personal authority of the holders of the great offices of state, such as the king. In this direction the argument sets its face against various feudal conceptions. The legitimacy or illegitimacy of the state can and must therefore be discussed in abstraction from the will of the people and from the personal and moral characteristics of the persons who exercise state-power.[41]

The rough historical parallelism in the three dimensions is obviously no accident, but one should not rush to make any naive assumptions about a purportedly mono-causal nature of the process as a whole, as if the idea or concept of the state were no more than an epiphenomenon, a mere reflection of endogenous processes of concentration and restructuring of social power. The reason one should hesitate to rush ahead in this way is that many of the more important forms of such restructuring presuppose that the agents in question already have the concept 'state', which on this mono-causal view should be a mere reflection of the changes they are about to initiate. It is equally obvious that people in the late sixteenth century did not simply invent a new concept 'state' out of full cloth, and then set out to bring the state into existence. In other words, there is no single, universal answer to the question 'which came first, the concept or the social reality?', except to reject that way of putting the question.

Skinner's account is *not* simply an observation about the real course of European history, and it is also most emphatically *not* the mere recounting of an odd fact about the history of language. Rather it has deep implications for the very possibility of asking general questions about authority and legitimacy in the political realm, for the particular way in which those questions arise for us, for the possible answers we can

---

[41] Skinner, 'The state', especially section 'v'.

envisage, and thus for the kind of social and political change that will be possible for us.

The approaches to the state I have just outlined, those of Weber, Marx, and Skinner, are in fact more or less extentionally equivalent in the modern world, but this may in the larger scheme of things be no more than a historical contingency. In most of the modern societies that are commonly recognised as 'states' a group of social specialists does (more or less) successfully monopolise legitimate violence. These specialists act on the basis of a warrant which gives them the power, by virtue of their occupying a certain position in an abstractly construed state-structure, to do what they need to do. Such entities are 'states' in Max Weber's sense. Equally clearly there could in principle be an institutionally distinct group of specialists who regulated distribution of economic surpluses and wielded some kind of military power *without* it being the case that such a group was perceived as inhabiting a distinct structure which itself needed separate legitimation. Thus perhaps certain temple economies in the ancient world are 'states' in Marx's but not in Skinner's sense. They may have organised production very effectively through a huge bureaucracy, but failed to make claims to a distinctly civil authority, different from religious authority. Clearly, too, there could be a successful monopolisation of legitimate violence exercised by some group of individuals 'personally', that is, so that it was not thought necessary for there to be a distinct authorisation of this by reference to a warrant associated with the holding of some abstract office. Perhaps ancient Sparta or certain early medieval political formations were 'states' in Weber's sense but not in Skinner's.

Finally the Nietzschean genealogist would point out that if 'the state' designates an inherently historical phenomenon, it will be impervious to formal definition, and will not have any one fixed 'nature' or 'essence' – one set of powers, structures, goals, purposes, or functions which never changes. As human purposes and beliefs change over time, one can expect these changes to find expression in human institutions. To say that the 'state' does not have a single defining function is not to say that at some given historical time some of its functions are not more important than others. Not only is this not an implication of the genealogical view, but it is in fact contrary to the spirit in which a genealogy is conducted. Nietzsche does not believe in fixed essences, but he is also *not* a liberal pluralist who sees history as a wide meadow on which an enormous number of unclassifiably various species of flowers can blossom without impinging on or interfering with each other. Rather, history is a free-for-all in which agents of varying size and internal constitution are attempting to subjugate *other* agents to their will. To subjugate another agent is to make that agent functionally serve my own ends. Institutions are part of this struggle.

The basic model for understanding history is the transformation of pre-existing social institutions like the hospital system, the educational system, the state, or the penal system when a new revolutionary government comes to power. A hospital system is at any given time a structured set of various powers, agents, functions, and goals. It may originally have been founded by a religious order who saw physical health as subordinate to salvation. In the course of the years, perhaps there was a gradual transformation of this conception into a more humanistic view. When the Bolsheviks or the National Socialists take power, what they try to do is to give the health system a new interpretation and a new meaning and turn it into a subordinate of their own goals. Instead of being an institution of Christian charity or liberal universalist humanitarianism, it is an instrument of the world proletarian revolution or a tool for the preservation of the health of a particular race. Such revolutionary processes are epistemically enlightening not because all of history is a series of revolutions or because only revolutionary change is important, but because in such revolutions one can see in a particularly condensed, accelerated, and self-conscious visible way the kind of thing which is happening less visibly, intensely, and quickly in all of history.

To be sure, such revolutionary projects do not always succeed, and they certainly do not abolish all the previous teleological structures embedded in the existing institution at a stroke. In characteristic cases the result will be a system in which older strata of meaning and powers will continue to exist in tension with, but also in subjection to, a dominant new set of goals and functions. To understand such a system is to both understand the multiplicity of its historically given internal structural features and the pre-eminence of whatever agency – whatever set of goals and powers – is dominant. The Nietzschean account has the great advantage of encouraging us to look with open eyes at the multiplicity of things the state does, the functions it serves, and the powers it has.

8. ANARCHY AND THE STATE

Not everyone in the twentieth century accepted the state as the unavoidable framework within which we must live. 'Anarchism' systematically rejected the legitimacy of the state, so studying anarchism will perhaps throw some light on what is involved in accepting the state and what the reasons for accepting it might be. As we shall see, one of the upshots of the discussion will be that the very idea of 'accepting the state' becomes less clear that it might initially seem.

'Anarchy' does not actually mean 'society lacking a state', but society without 'rule' or, as we would say, without political authority. In point of fact, anarchists generally rejected the moral authority of organised religions with as much or even greater vehemence than the claims of the political authorities. In general, anarchism seems to be rejection of any institutionally established and effective embodied claim to authority. Since the state is only one highly specific form that political authority can take, the anarchist's opposition to the state is merely the specific form which general opposition to all political authority will naturally take in the modern world, a place in which state-authority is the major form of authority which one will be likely to encounter. Nevertheless for the sake of simplicity I will treat the state as the main object of the anarchist's attack.

Anarchism can mean two slightly different things: there is 'real-life' anarchism and 'theoretical' or 'philosophical' anarchism'.[42] Real-life anarchism is the attempt to reorganise society so as to do without the state (or, more generally, without the notion and reality of political authority); thus it is tacitly committed to the view that such a society is both possible and desirable. Theoretical or philosophical anarchism is the negation of some view about the possible *de jure* legitimacy of the state, in the 'philosophical sense' of *de jure*. Given that theoretical anarchism is a negative philosophical view (the 'an' component of the word is the Greek privative), what it means will depend on the exact nature of the purported 'legitimacy' of the state which it claims to reject. Usually it is a view that as citizens or subjects we are under some strong moral obligation to obey a government or support the state.

The two forms of anarchism are conceptually distinct in that it is possible to be an anarchist in one sense without also being an anarchist in the other. Thus if the predominant view is that obedience to the state is a strict moral obligation of the Kantian sort, I can be a philosophical anarchist in denying that I am bound by any such obligation to obey the state, while still holding that it would be inadvisable to do away with the state. I might think the state useful and virtually indispensable without accepting specifically moral claims about it. Similarly for the purposes

---

[42] The best treatment of 'philosophical' anarchism is still that of R. P. Wolff, *In Defense of Anarchism*, second edition 1998 (University of California Press (first edition Harper & Row, 1970)) although his approach is vitiated by starting from an exceedingly idiosyncratic and narrow form of Kantian ethics.

of argument it is at least conceivable that I might think the state based on some kind of promise which binds those who made it and thus puts them under an obligation to obey its directives. I might think that in fact most people in society (including myself) had made such a promise and were now bound by it, but at the same time I might well think that it would be possible, good, and desirable for us to dissolve this structure of promises, release ourselves from this set of obligations, abolish the state, and structure political life differently.

Another way to see the two is as rejections of two alternative ways of construing the legitimacy of the state. Real-life anarchism denies that the state is, as the Kantian would put it, either categorically or hypothetically legitimate, that is, such anarchists deny that we stand under any binding obligation to form a state or enter into one which exists, or to obey one into whose power we have fallen. They also deny that the state is either unavoidable or highly desirable and that for this reason we ought to obey it. Theoretical anarchism is a rejection of a more highly moralised form of purported legitimation of the state, that it morally *ought* to exist or that when it does exist we are morally bound or obligated to obey it.

Max Weber provides a useful preliminary approach to real-life anarchism. He says that anarchism is the state of affairs in which 'the use of violence is unknown to social groups'. A full treatment of anarchism as a state of affairs should ideally comprise a discussion of four questions: (1) is anarchism a possible social form? (2) is it (possibly or under some conditions) a stable form? (And, if so, under what conditions?) (3) Is it accessible to us? (4) Would it be desirable? Obviously these questions are distinct from each other. A social form can be 'possible' in the short run, but highly unstable, or it can be stable, but not something directly accessible to us. Thus certain forms of organisation might be possible and stable only in societies with a small and relatively unchanging population. This would make them inaccessible to us in Western Europe, or rather not directly accessible, because they would require antecedent reduction in the population of the European Union from say 300 millions to a few dozen thousands. We probably could effect that kind of reduction given sufficient time, but we could not do it overnight (without violating some deeply held moral beliefs). So a society of the kind in question would not be a direct political option, although, of course, it equally does not follow from that that the image of such a society as an ideal would have no influence on actual political choices.

Although the four questions are distinct, the answers given to one will be closely related to those given to the others: clearly, for instance, few people will think a form of society is desirable if it is not minimally stable. It is also the case that thinking about these four questions and possible answers to them brings out in a striking way two fundamental features of politics. The first of these is the extent to which in politics 'moral' beliefs are connected to causal properties. Part of the reason why certain social forms are or are not 'stable' is that people in them do, or will, or would (or would not) find them acceptable; moral considerations play a very significant role in determining what counts as 'acceptable'. This in itself is a sufficient refutation of the so-called 'realist' approach to international politics.[43] The second is the extent to which notions of the desirable differ, and, in particular may change precisely as a result of our actions. When we ask: 'Would that society be desirable?' there are at least two answers to that question. (a) Would *we*, who are *now* considering moving from the present situation in which we live into the proposed utopian situation, like living in the utopia? This is itself a question to which there may be no unproblematic answer because of our deficient epistemic state, confusion about what we want, possible change of preferences over time, disagreement between those who constitute the 'we', and so on. (b) Assuming we were able, through political action, effectively to bring about the utopian situation would we *then* be pleased or satisfied with the life we would live? Large-scale political action, however, does not just change the world, it sometimes changes people's preference and moral views. It seems reasonable to give our present preferences and moral beliefs priority, but is it reasonable to give them absolute and exclusive priority? This re-educative effect that political action can have is of extreme importance, but it is also conceptually extremely intractable.

'A state of affairs in which the use of violence is unknown to social groups' can mean any one of four different things. First, it can mean that *any* form of violence, even the individual violence of one person against another, is completely unknown among members of the social group in question. Ethnologists have occasionally reported finding small human groups in which even individual violence was unknown, or at any rate minimal. Even if one takes these reports completely at face-value, it is striking that the societies in question have always been very small, very isolated groups with rudimentary economies and a very low technological level. It would at the very least require a powerful argument

---

[43] Hans Morgenthau, *Politics among Nations* (New York: Knopf, 1948). For a good recent treatment see M. Hollis and S. Smith, *Explaining and Understanding International Relations* (Oxford: Oxford University Press, 1990).

to claim that what might be possible for such groups could also be possible for a large and more integrated human society of the kind we now have in Western Europe (or indeed any kind of society that we could see would be even minimally attractive to the present inhabitants of the European Union).

The second sense of 'anarchism' is to designate a society which may have violence at an individual level – one farmer smacks another if he takes too much of the common lunch – but in which there is no social violence: one never sees groups of people attacking others. A society like this might be possible, although one would tend to think that it would require a very strong set of uniformly and widely held moral beliefs to prevent individual violence from becoming communal. It is also not at all clear that the kind of moral views it would require are ones that contemporary Europeans would find at all palatable. For instance, one fundamental component of such views would be that one should *not* help the weak if they are attacked by those who are stronger.

The third sense of 'anarchism' would be that although there is social violence, it is always informal. There are riots and lynchings, but no executions. There have been some who were sufficiently opposed to capital punishment to contrast judicially warranted execution *unfavourably* with murder, or at any rate with murder committed in a moment of passion. The coldly calculated nature of execution could be thought to be morally worse than straightforward murder. The murderer at least usually has the excuse of passionate personal involvement in the act and often does not bother hypocritically to claim that he or she is an agent of right, goodness, justice, or reason. For similar reasons, informal social violence (for example, the pogrom) could be thought to be morally less repellent than systematically organised forms (the concentration camp).[44]

The fourth sense of 'anarchism' designated a state in which although even organised violence might exist, such violence was not exercised by a 'state'. There might, then, be local individual self-help groups who might even have a certain internal organisation, but lacked the full properties of a state. Thus they might not have a distinct bureaucratic structure, or they might not successfully monopolise, or even claim to monopolise, the use of legitimate force, or finally they might not make any of the kinds of moral claims that states do. Historically anarchists were more concerned to reject the moral claims of the state than to oppose violence *per se*. To put it another way, it seems to have been psychologically easier for anarchists

---

[44] For discussion of one historical line of thought that leads to this (or the reverse) conclusion, cf. Albert Hirschmann, *The Passions and the Interests* (Princeton: Princeton University Press, 1977).

to accept a certain amount of human violence than to accept the claims of the state (and the church) to having a moral authority to prescribe forms of belief, exercise violence, and require obedience. With this, however, one slips over from real-life anarchism to philosophical anarchism.

9. THE LEGITIMACY OF THE STATE

The sense of 'legitimacy' that is at issue for philosophical anarchism is the one I have earlier[45] called '*de jure* legitimacy' in the philosophical sense. To ask whether the state is legitimate is to ask about the warrant state institutions have to command and the nature of the obligation under which individuals stand to obey these. I shall discuss this topic under three rubrics: (a) from the notion of rationality, (b) from the notion of benefits, and (c) from the notion of consent.[46]

One might claim that the state is legitimate because it is supremely rational that there be a state or because it is supremely rational for any individual to be an active member of a functioning state. Unfortunately the notion of 'rationality' is itself unclear and potentially ambiguous, so there will be various versions of this claim that will differ from each other considerably, depending on the notion of 'rationality' one uses.

Thus some philosophers have claimed that it is necessary to distinguish two senses of 'rational'. The first is one which construes 'rational' as a relational, or relative or conditional property. If I have evidence of this-or-that kind, then it is rational (relative to that body of evidence) to believe that thus-and-so is the case. If I step out of the house on a grey morning and see that the streets are wet, it is rational for me to believe it has been raining. This notion of rationality is very vividly in evidence in cases of instrumental reasoning. *If* I have these and these wants and beliefs, *then* it is rational to do this or that. If I were to like to eat hedgehogs, and were to have good reason for thinking that that dark patch at the back of the garden was a hedgehog, that might make it rational for me to try to catch it for dinner.

This relational property of rationality is sufficiently well known to us to be comfortable working with it, but a number of modern German philosophers, however, have claimed that the basic notion of rationality, or at any rate, one important component of the basic notion of rationality,

---

[45] Chapter 1, §5, pp. 41–2.
[46] The fullest and most philosophically astute recent discussion of the topics treated in this section is John Simmons, *Moral Principles and Political Obligations* (Princeton: Princeton University Press, 1979).

is one that designates an absolute or substantial property,[47] not a relational property. On this view, then, it makes sense to say that this-or-that way of living is inherently 'rational' (or 'irrational') and not simply 'rational' (or 'irrational') relative to some specified set of beliefs, projects, commitments, desires, etc. Thus in the ancient world various philosophers, it has been argued, believed that a political life of a certain type, the life of an active citizen in a πόλις, was not just rational in a conditional sense, that is, rational *if* you wanted to attain some *other* goal (i.e. military expansion, security, well-being, etc.) but that it was *in itself* a more rational way to live than any other way of living. One could try to transfer this view from the πόλις to the modern state. A final descendant of this approach is that of Hegel who thinks that life in a state is absolutely more rational than any other kind of life and uses a highly and self-consciously self-referential or reflective argument to support this conclusion. The state is supremely rational because it constitutes the framework within which rationality can best flourish. The argument is circular because it essentially asserts that the state is rational because it allows rationality to flourish. Hegel thinks that this circularity is not an objection, but his grounds for this belief are complex and probably not extractable from his general metaphysics.

The first possibility, then, is that one could try to show that the organisation of a society politically into a state was rational in some substantial (i.e. non-conditional) sense of 'rational'. An approach like this to the legitimacy of the state might seem especially appropriate because some people have thought it important to attribute to the state a power to command unconditionally, and a substantial notion of rationality might be thought to be more likely to ground such a power than any relational concept could.

One enormous difficulty which this line of argument faces is that, for whatever reason, we now have great difficulty even imagining any but a relational or conditional rationality. There is, however, also a further problem with this approach. Even if we could imagine an absolute or unconditional rationality, and could show that the existence of the state is

---

[47] The most vociferous proponents of this view are Adorno and Horkheimer, at least at certain points in their intellectual careers. They held that the ancient world had a firm 'substantive' conception of rationality, which comes gradually to disappear in the modern period, being replaced by ever expanding and ramifying forms of instrumental rationality. Cf. M. Horkheimer, *The Eclipse of Reason:*, M. Horkheimer and T. Adorno, *Dialektik der Aufklärung* (Frankfurt/M: Fischer Verlag, 1969). Most Kantians will also distinguish between 'counsels of prudence' (which it is held to be merely conditionally rational to act on) and the dictates of morality (which are held to instantiate an absolute rationality).

justified by reference to such an absolute rationality – and those are two huge if's – it is not clear that this would have the motivational force which was the original reason for asking the question about legitimacy in the first place. Suppose then that the state has a warrant issued by Absolute Rationality to give me orders, why should I obey? Those who have read (too much) Kant will be tempted to say: you should obey because if you do not you will show yourself to be irrational. What, though, is so wrong with being irrational?

One possibility is that absolute rationality has the property that it is literally unimaginable that one reject it, having once seen or recognised it. Or perhaps one can no more have reasons for failing to do what absolute rationality demands than one can have reasons to think that something is a square circle. This line of argument seems exceedingly unconvincing. Dostoyevky was not making a self-evidently incomprehensible statement when he wrote (in *Notes from Underground*) that sometimes humans might have an overriding interest in showing themselves precisely not to be the slaves of rationality, and thereby demonstrating the difference between being a human being and being a piano key. A prime candidate for inclusion in even the thinnest conception of 'absolute rationality' would be observance of the law of non-contradiction, but Montaigne was formulating a profound human truth, not excluding himself from the domain of the sane or showing that he was leading a poor, unhappy, or immoral life, when he wrote: 'Occasionally, to be sure, I may contradict myself, but the truth I never contradict.'[48] It does not follow from this, of course, that the observance of the law of non-contradiction is merely optional in practical contexts in which I am pursuing some goal (or, obviously, in well-defined, strictly theoretical contexts). Rationality in the pursuit of a goal seems, though, to be a form of conditional, not absolute rationality. In cases of conditional rationality, however, the motive I have for being rational is clear; violations of conditional rationality punish themselves. If I want and need A, and B is the only means to A, doing not-B will be associated with the sanction of not getting what I want and need. It is not at all clear that there is or could be any parallel notion of a sanction for possible violations of a non-conditional rationality, and thus what motivation I might have to conform to it.

Nietzsche gives a parallel analysis of truth, on the one hand, and reason/rationality, on the other, which seems to me to be inescapable. In both cases we can see perfectly comprehensible everyday usages that are

[48] M. Montaigne, *Essais*, ed. M. Rat (Paris: Garnier, 1962), vol. III, ch. 2 '*Du repentir*': 'Tant y a que je me contredits bien à l'aventure, mais la vérité . . . je ne la contredy point', p. 222.

embedded in contexts of instrumental action: we want to know whether it is true that this door leads to the lady (and that one to the tiger) because we want to get the lady and avoid the tiger. We want to use available techniques of reasoning to assess the evidence for the claim that this is the right door and that the wrong one, for similar obvious reasons. The philosophical tradition, however, has tended to extract both these concepts – truth and rationality – from their everyday instrumental context, absolutise each one and set it up as an object of aspiration not for the sake of instrumentally successful human action in the world, but as an unconditional end, something to be pursued for its own sake. When Nietzsche asks about the value of truth, a parallel question can be asked about the value of rationality. In particular why be 'unconditionally' rational, i.e. why pursue rationality in cases in which it is *ex hypothesi* disconnected from the usual motivational contexts which give it meaning?

If the whole idea of an 'absolute' or utterly unconditional rationality does not make much sense, and in any case would have a doubtful motivational effect, perhaps one would have better luck with a conditional conception of rationality. Any approach that uses such a conditional conception, though, must immediately say what the goal or end is to which the state is the rational means. Historically one of the most frequently pursued variants of this approach has been one that assumes that the state should be viewed as if it were an artifice[49] which is constructed in order to attain a single goal. One of the most frequently posited goals for the state is security. Security can be taken in a more or a less extensive sense. In the minimal sense it would mean the security of my life, my mere continued biological existence. In a more extensive sense it could include my bodily integrity, my freedom of motion, or certain forms of minimal absence of humanly inflicted pain. A very extensive reading might include the security of my 'property' (in some sense of that term that was further to be specified).

The argument, then, would run as follows: giving the state a warrant to command and imposing on its members an obligation to obey is a means which allows the state to ensure or enhance the security of its members. Thus the state form in general would be seen to be conditionally rational because and to the extent to which it ensured the security of its members, and any particular state would have legitimacy to the extent to which it employed its power to command in order effectively to maintain 'security' (in whatever was deemed to be the appropriate sense of that term).

---

[49] T. Hobbes, *Leviathan*, ed. R. Tuck (Cambridge: Cambridge University Press, 1996) (2nd edition), p. 9.

Obviously not every political association that satisfied Weber's definition of a state would also satisfy this condition of legitimacy. Weber's definition merely asserts that for a state to exist there must be an agency that successfully monopolises legitimate violence (in a given geographic area). This might be interpreted to mean that the agency in question was capable of preventing *other* competing agencies from using violence within a certain territory, but it by no means implies that the agency *itself* does not threaten the security of its own members. That is, France is a state if it can prevent Belgian authorities from legitimately beating up people in Lille, but that is compatible with the French state itself being sufficiently internally repressive to constitute a danger to its citizens and inhabitants, either directly by the classic forms of torture, and execution, or indirectly, by encouraging the use of the motor car, permitting uncontrolled genetic modification of food, building unsafe nuclear reactors, and so on.

Adopting this approach would seem to require a shift in our usual conception of legitimacy. On this account it would seem that the only warrant the state would have would be for actions directly conducive to security; this would tend to limit the realm of obedience significantly. In addition, security seems to be a matter of degree. Is, then, political obligation to obey the directives of the state not just conditional, but also proportional to the degree of actual security provided?[50]

The Nietzschean approach to the state I have been promoting forces one, as I have already mentioned, to qualify to some extent the assumption on which this line of argument is based. If Nietzsche is right the state is not best and most fully understood as a teleological entity directed exclusively at attaining some single end or as having a single function. This is true even if that single end is a 'security' which is an accordion concept, contracting sometimes to designate bare biological existence, but also expandable to encompass increasingly complex and sophisticated forms of personal and social welfare. Thus, in addition to providing security, the state might regulate the economy, provide a focus for feelings of self-worth, predictably structure a variety of kinds of human sociability, serve as a central point for the collection and distribution of information, and for the coordination of various kinds of actions, and so on.

If, then, states are historically continuous entities that serve a variety of different ends, this complicates any analysis of the (conditional) rationality of giving the state a warrant to command, or of the grounds an

[50] Cf. John Dunn, 'Political Obligation', in his *The History of Political Theory and Other Essays* (Cambridge: Cambridge University Press, 1996).

individual member of the society might have for taking the commands of the state into account as having normative standing in their own right. There might be rather different warrants for different kinds of commands, and the grounds any individual might have for accepting some command as authoritative might be a composite of a variety of different considerations.[51]

I mentioned at the beginning of this section that the concept of rationality was not completely univocal, and I have discussed briefly one way in which that is the case by contrasting conditional with absolute conceptions of rationality. There is, however, another aspect to this ambiguity in that 'rationality' can designate either a systemic property of a form of political organisation as a whole, or a subjective motivational property of an individual agent. That is, any relatively informed observer may make the systemic judgement that (given some end in view) it is rational for the large-scale food stocks of a certain society to be preserved intact as provision against unexpected natural disasters. It might nevertheless be perfectly rational for an individual woman in the society who is hungry to try to pilfer enough to satisfy her immediate hunger; after all, if the stock is sufficiently great, she may (quite correctly) think that the little she will eat will save her from great present discomfort, but represent a virtually invisible diminution of the provision.

This discrepancy between a systemic and an agent-centred sense of 'rationality' characterises a class of goods that has been of great importance for politics. These goods are non-divisible and have the property that if they are provided at all, they must be provided jointly to all the members of a given group. Thus a certain street is either paved and lighted or it is not, and if it is, it is for all those who live on the street.[52] It may, then, be rational for all who live on this street to pool together to pay for installing and maintaining a pavement and a system of lights. Yet it may also be rational for any individual to attempt to free-ride, to enjoy the benefits of the public services in question, while avoiding paying for them. If only a very small number of people fail to pay their contribution to the pool, the public services can continue to operate on the funds available, but at a certain point, if the number of delinquents

---

[51] I take this to be the upshot of the exceedingly astute analysis one finds in Joseph Raz's *Morality of Freedom*.

[52] What will have this property of jointness of supply will depend to a great extent on technology. If we had a different technology, perhaps it would be possible for the street to be light and paved when I walked down it, but dark and unpaved when someone else walked down it. Discussion of this and related issues was initiated by Mancur Olson in *The Logic of Collective Action: Public Goods and the Theory of Groups* (Cambridge, Mass.: Harvard University Press, 1965).

gets sufficiently large, the system will collapse. This means that it might be rational in a further sense for all those involved to institute a system of coercion which through threat of punishment would ensure that a sufficient number of people paid their contribution to allow the system to continue to function.[53] Under such a system it might still be rational for me to try to evade payment, provided that the chances of being caught were sufficiently remote, the envisaged punishment in the case of detection sufficiently trivial, and the likelihood of my causing others to emulate my action sufficiently low.[54] In principle, then, one could come to the conclusion that it might be rational for us to grant the state a warrant to issue categorical commands and to enforce them in various ways (including the use of coercion) and in that sense we could affirm that the state structure was legitimate, and yet it might still be an open question whether or not it was rational for an individual agent to conform to these commands.

A second argument for the legitimacy of the state appeals to the notion of benefits received. This argument has a different structure from the previous one. The previous appeal to the conditional rationality of obeying the state because of possible benefits was a prospective argument: I obey now in order to obtain those (or raise my chances of obtaining them). This argument is retrospective and depends on some notion of a moral obligation of gratitude for past benefits conferred. There seem to be a number of obvious and immediate difficulties with this approach. First of all, benefits are highly differentially distributed in society, and this might suggest that political obligation was equally differentially distributed. In fact, if that were the case the least advantaged in society would be under the lightest obligation, a thought that would have rather significant implications in a wide variety of areas, not least public security in urban areas. The second difficulty is that it does seem at least a bit odd to be thought to be under an obligation of gratitude for 'benefits' which one has received without asking for them and without even any particular consultation of one's preferences. In addition, gratitude is usually thought to designate an open-ended psychological attitude which is not necessarily correlated with any specific response. If a transaction involves a concrete, specific *quid pro quo* the terms of which are stipulated beforehand we generally think of it as a kind of economic exchange, i.e. as the

53 See J. Elster, *Ulysses and the Sirens: Studies in Rationality and Irrationality* (Cambridge: Cambridge University Press, 1979) on the rationality of introducing restrictions on fully free decision.
54 Cf. Richard Tuck, 'Why is Authority such a Problem?', in *Philosophy, Politics, and Society* ed. P. Laslett, W. G. Runciman, and Q. Skinner. Fourth Series (Oxford: Blackwell, 1972).

kind of thing for which categories like gratitude are not self-evidently appropriate. Even if I accept that I ought to feel a general sense of gratitude
to my society and its political order for the benefits they have conferred
on me in the past, it is hard to see how that can be transformed into any
very particular attitude I should have towards a specific directive.

   That leads to the final strand of argument, from the notion of consent.
This general line of argument is one that has historically been of some
theoretical importance in the West, lying as it does behind the 'social
contract' approach. The basic intuition is that the state is legitimate because I have consented to obey it and be governed by it. Thus it has a
warrant to command me which I have given it; it ought to be able to
expect me not just to give its directives some normative weight, but to
conform to its orders to the letter. Philosophers have sometimes appealed
to the model of promising or contracting in order to give concreteness
to this abstract claim about 'consent'. To be sure, a powerful tradition
in sociology, descending in particular from the work of Durkheim,[55]
has pointed out repeatedly that 'promising' is a highly specific social practice, and that the 'contract' is not a free-standing structure that could exist
prior to society, but rather a peculiar institution which depends heavily
on the antecedent existence of a set of other well-entrenched, regulatory
social institutions and is unthinkable in their absence. Since this is the
case, they have argued, it is a mistake to try to construe the most basic
institutions and structures of society as if they resulted from promising or
contracting. The more sophisticated philosophers in the social contract
tradition have replied by granting but trying to deflect this point. What
is at issue here, they have asserted, is not society as a whole, but the state
as a very particular way of structuring a society politically, so the fact that
contract is not sociologically fundamental for understanding the way in
which society as a whole holds itself together is irrelevant.

   Philosophers who try to derive legitimacy from consent claim, then,
that I am bound by political obligations because I have promised, or
have entered into, or could be thought of as having entered into, a social
contract with the other members of my society by which we bind ourselves to mutual obedience (under appropriate circumstances, i.e. when
the orders are correctly issued). Despite its historical (and contemporary) influence and visibility, this line seems such a non-starter that it is
hard to keep one's attention focused on possible grounds for it rather
than on trying to determine for what historical or sociological reason

[55] E. Durkheim, *La division du travail social* (Paris: PUF, 1986).

something so implausible could ever have been taken seriously for such a long time.

Of the various kinds of objections to this line of argument I will focus on two, each of which seems to me overwhelmingly plausible. First of all, a promise or a contract may not be something that is expressed in an explicit *verbal* form, but still it seems that it must make sense to ask at what time and in what place the promise was made or the contract entered into. It does not seem to make much sense to ask when or where I promised or contracted to obey any of the particular states in whose jurisdiction I have happened to find myself. The usual strategy is to shift from our normal notions of promising (when I *say* that I promise) or contracting (when I pronounce a formula or sign a document of some kind) to some notion of tacit promising or contracting. I am then thought tacitly to have promised or contracted by virtue of performing certain actions such as paying taxes, voting, allowing myself to be elected to public office, and so on.

The difficulty with this is that many of the actions cited by theories of this kind as evidence of a tacit promise or contract are no such things. I give no promise to the government when I engage in everyday actions like buying and selling provisions, which will be necessary under any political regime. Even more strictly 'political' acts may have *some* utilitarian value, such as allowing myself to be elected to the local Council, although in many countries this will be a highly dubious example of an action with utilitarian value. Why must I be thought to have made any promises, if I make use of an instrument or institution that is useful? In addition, in many countries people may be subject to very forceful 'encouragement' to participate on the part of the authorities; one might, for instance, need to have voted in order to get certain benefits, like a place for one's children in higher education. Under these circumstances many people may feel they have no choice but to participate in a political process which they in no way think has 'legitimacy' in any normative sense. Another possibility is that those subject to the prevailing authorities may participate and have no view whatever about the legitimacy of the political structure. People may assume that it is just *there*, perhaps like a natural nuisance that must be dealt with in one way or the other, or they may give it the kind of (merely *de facto*) recognition of 'legitimacy' one country gives another with whom it sees it must *nolens volens* deal.

It is hard to see how any such actions can count as giving a promise of obedience or making a contract, since they are explicitly consistent with thinking that the regime in question is utterly reprehensible and unworthy. To put it another way, part of the point of this approach to legitimacy is presumably to distinguish between a kind of acceptance which indicates consent or minimal affirmation of a regime, on the one hand, and mere stoical tolerance of something that one is afraid of or sees no realistic way to avoid, on the other. The *less*, however, one requires some explicit verbal affirmation of consent, the more difficult it becomes to distinguish 'tacit consent' from mere toleration, and the more focused coercion there is in the society the less even explicit expressions of consent can be taken at face-value. It is at least arguable that the more reprehensible the regime, the less I should feel myself bound by any formal or tacit promises extracted from me. Of course, one could say that to the extent to which people do even passively tolerate a regime they have consented to it. Then, at least, distinct passive resistance or active insurrection become the signs of lack of consent. Given that most modern regimes will take measures against even relatively passive resistance, it will require a certain amount of courage and persistence to deny consent. If one took this line, one would be very much in danger, then, of returning to a kind of Hobbesian view wherein failing effectively to disrupt political life is tantamount to being bound to obey. Presumably, however, the whole point of the exercise of introducing the notion of 'consent' was precisely to distinguish between regimes that satisfied the Weberian criterion of *actually* effectively monopolising the use of legitimate violence, and regimes that were 'legitimate' in some further sense that had moral standing. To the extent to which consent is allowed to be tacit it becomes more and more difficult to make this distinction.

The second objection to the purported derivation of legitimacy from consent is that we usually think that 'consent' is something that must be freely given if it is to have any standing, and to say it is freely given must mean that the agent has some choice in the matter. In the modern world I may have a choice of different regimes, but I do not really and effectively have the choice of living wholly outside the context of a state. States of one kind or another have now divided up the surface area of the globe, and their jurisdiction is *imposed* – if you happen to be in Fiji, you are subject to the laws of Fiji, whether you want to be or not. This makes it extremely difficult to see how anything I might do, short of swearing allegiance in completely free circumstances, would count as an exercise of free and voluntary choice or consent in a sense that could be thought to give rise to an obligation.

With the masts broken off, the timbers sprung, the seas washing over the deck, and all hands lost overboard, some philosophers, clinging to bits of wreckage bobbing up and down in the swell, have still tried heroically to claim that the ship really is afloat, on course, and making headway. The 'promise' or 'consent' in question, they have claimed, is not *real* consent, but hypothetical consent. Conceptually 'hypothetical' consent is different from the 'tacit' consent discussed earlier. 'Tacit' consent purports to refer to some real state of affairs in which I *have* given consent, although I have not *expressed* that consent directly. Thus, I may be said tacitly to have consented to participation in some action, if, when given ample opportunity to stop or object, I fail to do that and continue. Hypothetical consent does not purport to refer to what I now do consent to in the real circumstance or have consented to, but to what I would consent to in some other circumstances. It is not that I have consented or do consent (even tacitly) to be governed by the state, but that under 'ideal' conditions I *would* consent, or that under certain ideal circumstances it can be seen that it would be reasonable for me to consent. This hypothetical contract is claimed to be sufficient to bind me, and require me to obey. In hypothetical circumstances I might, of course, indeed consent to any number of things, but how am I supposed really to be bound in the political world by a merely hypothetical promise it might be reasonable for me to make under the circumstances specified by a highly artificial thought-experiment?

The state itself – that is, any given state – obviously has a vested interest in presenting itself not just as an agency that discharges a variety of different functions and provides certain services, and one whose commands it is rational for its members to take seriously, but one that ought *categorically* to be obeyed. It would be highly convenient for those who benefit from state-power if we were to believe that we stood in a deep moral relation to it which we could break only at our peril. It is, then, not surprising that functionaries of the state and their paid and unpaid theorists try to induce this belief. None of the arguments canvased above, though, gives grounds for accepting it.

Is philosophical anarchism then correct? Yes and no. It is true that *if* one construes 'anarchism' as the doctrine that there can be no categorical quasi-moral justification which binds me under absolutely all circumstances to obey all the formally correct directives of a regime I consider legitimate, then that is right. The proper general conclusion to be drawn from this discussion, however, is that this Kantian way of posing the question of 'legitimacy' is naive. Although there is no categorical imperative, there can still be any number of good reasons that should move people to support political institutions that give the occupants of certain positions the power to issue directives, and there can be very good reasons for people generally to obey these directives. There can even be good grounds to say that people 'ought' to obey the directives, although not that they ought 'categorically' (or 'absolutely') to obey. These grounds can include habit, networks of reciprocal expectations, solidarity, certain benefits the state provides, moral views about how individuals ought to act, calculations of systemic rationality, gratitude, etc. It can even be thought that these grounds ought reasonably to outweigh considerations of narrow personal advantage in some cases.

Philosophical anarchism is itself infected with the disease against which it thinks itself the cure. Its rejection of the moralising claims of the state (and church) make sense only if one takes these claims at face value. If one had really freed oneself from Christianity and its successors (including Kant), from the whole concept of absolute obligation, the fact that the state was incapable of placing us under an 'absolute obligation' would come as no surprise, and would not be grounds for criticising it (only its self-conception). The traditional anarchist agrees to play the 'all or nothing' game the Kantian proposes: either categorical obligation or *Willkür* (arbitrary choice). The anarchist gives a different answer from the Kantian, but I wish to suggest that one would be better advised to reject these terms of play altogether.

The real difficulty with anarchism is not with its philosophical, but with its real-life form. It is not that people are convinced of the philosophical validity of arguments for the obligation to obey the state, but rather that no one really believes we can now do without something like a state structure. Or rather people imagine that the attempt to do away with the state would lead in one of two directions. The first possibility would be a form of society that would be highly dangerous, unpredictable, and insecure, and would lack many of the economic advantages developed industrial societies have. The only alternative would be a society that would be highly repressive because organised into claustrophobic small groups, and in which one would have the unpleasant sense of living in the unventilated atmosphere of a Jane Austen novel all the time.[56]

---

[56] See Michael Taylor, *Community, Anarchy, and Liberty* (Cambridge: Cambridge University Press, 1982).

CHAPTER 2

Liberalism

I. THE CONTEXT

For a number of reasons and in a number of ways liberalism is conceptually and theoretically much more elusive than the state. For one
thing, a given state, after all, is a set of concrete social institutions,
which has an aspect of sheer facticity in the form of customs posts,
national assembly buildings, oaths of allegiance, aircraft carriers flying
the state's flag, postage stamps, police stations with stacks of rubber trun-
cheons and cattle prods, printed law books, official seals, and so forth.
Liberalism is more like Christianity than like the state, that is, it is a
complex of doctrines, ideals, suggestions for implementing those ideals,
beliefs, and informal patterns of habitual action and thought. Liberalism,
though, is both much more doctrinally amorphous and indeterminate
than Christianity was, and has a much more indirect relation to any social reality. Christianity had its church buildings, rituals, *symbola*, public
professions of faith, seminaries, catechisms, and, at least at some points
in its history, inquisitorial tribunals, prisons, etc. The prisons of liberalism are prisons of the mind, and they operate by trapping the unwary
in a shifting, labyrinthine hall of mirrors rather than by immobilisation
behind palpable brick and steel.

Like the state and Christianity, liberalism is something that had (and
has) a history – it has changed and developed over time, partly in response to observation of the actual effects of its own actions etc. It is not,
however, a fossil, but still a vital, politically, morally, and ideologically engaged movement which struggles for influence on the minds and actions
of modern populations. That liberalism is such a practically engaged,
historically located phenomenon has three important and interrelated
consequences: (a) it has no definition, (b) it tends to rewrite its own past,
sometimes anachronistically, (c) it is open to very significant modification
in the future.

The first of these three consequences is merely a reiteration of the general Nietzschean point I made earlier.[1] If liberalism is in the first instance a real historical movement, which has been characterised by differing collections of sometimes rather vague and ill-defined beliefs, commitments, concerns, and projects at different times, then, although no one can stop a theorist from trying to 'define' his or her private brand of liberalism by a set of abstract propositions, and declaring that this is what liberalism 'really' is, that is not the most enlightening way to understand it. 'Liberalism' in the present is whatever you can get enough people to agree is 'in the spirit' of or continuous with a tradition, which was itself composed of a number of distinct strands.

The second consequence of the proposed understanding of liberalism concerns the relation of liberalism to its past. Because liberalism is an active player in the world of politics – attempting to marshal support and gain power – not a fossil, it has an interest in presenting its own past in a particular way, emphasising continuities with those features of the past that will make it seem attractive, and downplaying those that might tend to reflect badly on it, so one can expect a certain amount of mystification about its nature and past especially on the part of contemporaries who consider themselves liberals. One particular form this mystification can take is anachronism.

The danger of historical anachronism, then, is at least as severe in the study of 'liberalism' as in that of 'the state'. Given that in our world we have the concept 'state', which we use to refer to a very distinct, highly important, virtually omnipresent, almost palpable part of it, we find it hard to conceive of a society that lacks this reality. We are tempted to project the concept back on to previous societies even when in some sense we know they did not have anything corresponding to it. Even in the fourth-century Athenian πόλις we look for a 'state'.[2] The situation is not exactly the same for a phenomenon like 'liberalism'. To be sure, one can trawl extant historical literature in search of anticipations of the liberal temper, but almost anyone can see that the catch will be very meagre until the eighteenth century. The pre-history of the concept ends in about 1810 when there comes to be a political party (in Spain) that explicitly *calls itself* 'The Liberal Party', and then 'liberalism' comes to be used to refer to the doctrines and attitudes of parties like that; one can eventually speak of 'a liberal society'. 'A liberal society' can mean a society liberals would approve of, or, alternatively, the kind of society

[1] See above, Introduction, pp. 6–10.
[2] See above, p. 44.

that would result if one put liberals' political projects into effect; these two things can differ because, given the unpredictability of the outcome of human action, the society that would eventuate from implementing liberal ideals might not be a society of which liberals would then approve. Finally a 'liberal' society could mean one that would be likely to give rise to characteristically liberal concerns and attitudes and thus render liberalism a plausible political position. Liberalism, however, seems virtually born looking backward and usurping, or at any rate claiming for itself on exceedingly weak grounds, a much older ancestry than a historian of the strictest discipline would perhaps be willing to attest for it. Thus, Locke is routinely listed among the purported progenitors, and sometimes this list is extended back even to encompass Spinoza.

The third consequence refers to the future of 'liberalism'. If a concept like 'liberalism' does not designate anything that has a fixed essence, only a history, then it will *always* be unclear where its extension ends.[3] Any concept can in principle and in fact always be extended beyond its usual range; there is no antecedently fixed limit to this process. 'Liberalism' in the future, then, will be anything one can get out of that history by warping it appropriately. The warping could take place in a variety of different ways, some of them incompatible with each other. However, although one can in principle transform liberalism into something very different from what it was in the past or is now, it does not follow that one can do that equally easily in any direction at any time and, most importantly, the transformation cannot be effected at a single stroke. The historical starting point thus does not absolutely define and determine what liberalism is and can be, but it is also not irrelevant to understanding where it can easily end up, and in which directions it will be easier, in which more difficult to move it. If I set out on foot now from Cambridge, there is no limit in principle to where in the mainland UK I could eventually end up, but that does not imply that I can start walking now and reach Land's End tomorrow. Knowing about where concepts come from, how they have been used, what past power relations and intentions have been impressed on them, and have left their mark on them, does not either strictly tell us how we *must* use them. We are, within limits, free to expand, modify, or change their mode of usage in any of a variety of directions. This knowledge also does not enable us to detach ourselves completely from the history of our concepts, if only because we still need

---

[3] Nietzsche expresses this by denying that there is a clear distinction between a literal and metaphorical usage of a concept. See *Über Wahrheit und Lüge in einem außermoralischen Sinne* in *Kritische Gesamt-ausgabe*, vol. I and also *Zur Genealogie der Moral*, vol. V.

to use the terms we have in something like their recognisable senses in order to communicate with others. Nevertheless this knowledge may be a form of power.

Just as one cannot identify 'liberalism' once and for all with any single sharply etched theoretical statement which is taken to define it, so similarly one cannot simply take some one brief historical period or figure or group and baptise it 'true liberalism'. Or rather, as in the case of the definition, no one can stop me from doing this if I wish and if the particular purpose of my enquiry makes this seem reasonable, but the results of such a procedure are likely to be less than optimally useful if what one is seeking is a general understanding of liberalism. The Nietzschean attack on essentialism was not intended as a licence for intellectual laziness – don't bother to try to make any generalisations about liberalism; it is vague and shifting doctrine, and has no essence anyway. Generalisations are indispensable intellectual tools. The canonical text in which Nietzsche is most forthcoming about methodological issues, *Zur Genealogie der Moral*, is full of generalisations, including historical generalisations. There is good reason, then, to think that Nietzsche himself saw his attack on essentialism as fully compatible with acknowledging the obvious fact that we humans could not get along without generalisations. To think that the rejection of essentialism must imply abandoning the use of generalisations altogether, is to have accepted the view Nietzsche is arguing against, namely the view that a true generalisation *must* be understood in an essentialist way. Equally the fact that liberalism has a long and variable history does not mean one cannot pick out certain figures and movements as being of greater continuing importance for understanding it than others are.

The main theoretical and conceptual resources of liberalism are best understood, I claim, as originally arising from a two-fold movement, as part of a war on two fronts, at the end of the eighteenth and beginning of the nineteenth century. On one of the two fronts Humboldt rejected the older cameralist conception that the goal of the state is the welfare of its subjects and that the state thus has an obligation to provide for that welfare.[4] In place of this Humboldt propounded the minimalist conception of the state as a night watchman, and and claimed that the aim of

---

[4] Since the work by Humboldt which was of the greatest influence on the history of liberalism is one he wrote in the 1790s (*Ideen zu einem Versuch die Grenzen der Wirksamkeit des Staats zu bestimmen*; the most widely available edition of this is that published by Reclam (Stuttgart, 1967)) at which time there was no organised liberalism as a political movement and no concept 'liberalism' – in fact the terms 'liberal/liberalism' do not occur in this work by Humboldt – I am myself committing the sin of anachronism I excoriate in others.

human life was individual self-activity. The other front is that on which Constant struggled against what he took to be the excessively and inappropriately moralising conception of politics which established itself at the end of the eighteenth century. This conception took the specific form in Rousseau of a commitment to the state as the possible embodiment of a single, unitary, popular will and thus as locus of an overwhelming moral authority; for Robespierre it was to be embodied in the 'republic of virtue (and terror)', and for Kant in an abstract and rigid puritanical ethic as the foundation of politics. Over the following two hundred years four main elements of liberal thought emerge. To repeat, these four strands or principles or elements are not to be understood as sharply defined fixed propositions, but rather as vaguely defined tendencies or predilections that can be specified concretely in a number of different ways, and enter into historically complex relations with each other and with other beliefs and values, forming different constellations of what is more central and what is less central to liberalism; these will vary according to time and place.

First of all, liberalism is committed to some version of a principle of toleration, that is to the view that absence of systematic persecution of non-violently deviant modes of living is one of the cardinal virtues of a human society, and especially of the political order of society. A second complex of characteristically liberal views revolves around a certain conception of the nature and social role of freedom. Freedom of a certain kind is thought to be a central value, and liberals show a striking predilection for the voluntary as a basis for as many human social relations as possible, in particular holding that (free) consent is the only acceptable ground of political obligation. The third feature is two-headed: it emphasises on the one hand individualism and on the other autonomy, that is, it holds that the agents in the society should decide what they want to do as much as possible for themselves even if this goes against existing social expectations and patterns of thought, preference, and behaviour. Fourthly and finally, liberalism is characterised by a persistent suspicion of absolute, excessive, unlimited, or discretionary power.

2. TOLERATION

To start with the first strand in liberalism, the 'toleration' to which it is committed was originally negative, and referred specifically to religious policy. To say that it was a 'negative' concept means that there was no implication that the absolute truth in matters of religion was not known, nor was there an assumption that the existence of diversity had any positive value. There was no question of providing actual encouragement for deviancy, only of mitigating or limiting the negative sanctions to be imposed on it. In the early modern period there seem to have been three kinds of consideration that moved people in the direction of toleration: religious, humanistic–sceptical, and strictly political.

The religious argument derived directly from some elements in Christianity that became especially prominent in Protestantism.[5] These include in particular the view that the human soul was inviolably free in matters of belief, and thus that external coercion was doomed to failure. Other strands held that only completely free human belief had any value. These two lines of thought do not obviously fit together comfortably because to say that only free belief has value would seem to make sense only if one can sensibly contrast free belief with coerced belief, but if all belief is free, it is unclear how the contrast is to be made. If one took this general Protestant line, however, one could try to argue that attempts at coercion of *belief* were self-refuting in that even if they were to succeed, what they produced (coerced pseudo-belief) would be without religious value. Not all Christians, of course, drew this conclusion, and a number of them specifically rejected it. One could object to this defence of toleration for one or the other of two reasons. First, one could believe that it depended on a misleading lack of clarity about the differential standing and consequences of coercion for the individual(s) coerced and for the society as a whole. Second, one could think that it was based on much too naive a simple dichotomy between freedom and coercion.

To start with the first of these two objections, it might well be the case that people would be more likely to come freely to accept God in the right way if they were living in a religiously coherent, homogeneous social world (even if that cohesion was politically produced by coercive means), and lack of uniformity might mean the pointless unsettling of people who otherwise would be happy to continue to live in the truth. So although coercion might not work on the individual deviant, the social results of the execution or isolation of heretics – that is, proper social uniformity of belief – might be positive. Especially if one believed that such a deviant was irremediably damned anyway, the authorities might have a clear obligation to protect others from confrontation with something that might disturb them, but which was known to be of no conceivable real value to them (religious error). Social uniformity might

---

[5] See John Dunn, 'The Claim to Freedom of Conscience', in *The History of Political Theory and Other Essays* (Cambridge: Cambridge University Press, 1996).

make it easier to retain a faith freely acquired. This view still puts absolute value, finally, on individual salvation through having the right kind of faith, but thinks that social uniformity is the best means to attaining that goal for as many individuals as possible; the value of social conformity is thus construed as instrumental. This is different from another possible view one might hold, namely that living in an externally uniform society which conformed to divine injunctions and could be seen by its own members and others as so doing, was itself an independent (perhaps a transcendental) good of which everyone would be deprived by the toleration of deviance.

To turn to the second kind of objection, it might well also be the case, as Pascal perhaps thought, that certain kinds of belief/faith *can* be produced and are of value in individuals even though they are produced by coercion. 'Allez à la messe et la foi vous viendra.' This might not strictly be a case of strict or complete 'coercion' because it might be thought to presuppose that the decision to go to mass, at any rate, was minimally voluntary. It would be a case of voluntarily subjecting myself to conditions which I knew or hoped would change my beliefs. This has sometimes been called 'character planning';[6] there is nothing in principle paradoxical about it. Whether or not it is in fact possible to engage in character planning of a particular kind would depend on the kind of belief in question and also the kind of coercion. It might be significantly easier for me to decide that I wish to coerce myself into forming certain beliefs (and to be successful) than for me to form a belief as the result of being coerced by someone else, but the latter might not be impossible.

The 'Protestant' emphasis on interior freedom cannot be thought by itself to settle the issue of toleration definitively in any case precisely because of the sharp split it accepts between the interior human realm – that of belief, faith, conscience – and the external realm of human action. If only inner assent is important and of any value, and such assent is always completely free and distinct from external action, then why not conform externally, and why not permit a coercion in externals which by hypothesis will be religiously irrelevant? If only my inner state of will is important, what does it matter if I bow down to the Baal, as long as I distance myself from it internally in the appropriate way? What difference, then, does it make whether or not people are forced to perform the acts of sacrifice to idols? There might, then, be a religious argument for not enforcing *belief*, but that would not necessarily tell secular authorities

---

[6] See Elster, *Sour Grapes*.

anything about toleration of external behaviour. We rightly focus on the role of monotheistic religions in fostering certain kinds of specifically religiously motivated persecution,[7] and in general on producing an atmosphere in which intellectual and moral repression is more easily exercised and legitimated, and see in this their greatest historical significance. It should, however, also not be overlooked that for centuries governments have had what they thought were good political and social (not religious) reasons for preferring religious homogeneity. Maintenance of public order might be thought to be easier in a religiously homogeneous society; the national economy might be considered to benefit from economies of scale in provision of ministers, church buildings, and so on. Removal of religiously based arguments for enforcing conformity need not in any way make it politically less desirable (although it might make it less *feasible*) to pursue a policy of repression in the interests of religious homogeneity.

The second major form of argument for toleration which might persuade some people of the merits of a policy of negative toleration comes from a view about the proportionality between means and ends. Such a view might be rooted in a certain kind of (perhaps revived) ancient humanism, which puts great emphasis on moderation and the avoidance of excess or extremes. In some thinkers in the early modern period this can come to be coupled with a certain scepticism about the degree of certitude one can attain in religious and metaphysical affairs. If one thinks it hard to be absolutely sure about matters of religion *and* thinks that one should not use drastic coercive means in cases in which one is not sure, then it seems to follow that one ought not to coerce people in matters of religious belief. However, as various religiously minded thinkers (including Pascal and Kierkegaard) quickly pointed out, even if one accepted some version of the principle of commensurateness of means to end, this should be applied not to the degree of certainty alone, but to some combination of the degree of certainty *and* the inherent significance of the choice to be made. Perhaps I should not coerce people in trivial cases on evidence that fails to be absolutely convincing, but is it so obvious that I ought not to coerce in cases where the issue is of infinite importance (such as the salvation of a soul)? In fact this line of argument becomes convincing only if people *both* become sceptical about the possibility of knowledge in matters of religion *and* come to believe they are not overwhelmingly important. In the terms of Pascal's famous wager, what a possible god would have to offer would be only a form of

---

[7] Cf. Assman, *Moses the Egyptian*.

salvation that might be *very* pleasant indeed (and damnation that would be finitely unpleasant), but not something the acquisition of which would be overwhelmingly good (and the loss of which would be infinitely bad).

As Kierkegaard was to point out later with memorable vividness,[8] Christian religious belief (or faith) is on the one hand self-validating from the internal perspective. Once you have it you know that it is objectively true with complete certainty (although paradoxically the content of the truth is also what Kierkegaard calls 'subjectivity'). On the other hand, it is always inadequately motivated, when seen from the outside, i.e. from the point of view of someone who does not have it. To have faith is of absolute, in fact strictly transcendental importance – so much more important that nothing else has any significance at all compared with it. To realise that this is the case, however, already requires one to have faith, that is, an antecedent passionate commitment which informs all one's cognitive judgements in a certain way. If one does not already believe, one cannot appreciate the importance of belief. Thus, Kierkegaard claims that to adopt a purportedly neutral position – one which abstracts from faith – is to adopt a position from which the value of faith is invisible. To adopt a purportedly neutral position is already to have adopted an inherently non-religious position. So there is no genuinely neutral standpoint between believers and non-believers, one that did not pre-empt the outcome of the discussion, and there could not in principle be such a standpoint when fundamental questions concerning the whole of human existence are at issue. Although for historical reasons I bring up this denial of the possibility of neutrality with respect to specifically religious views, it is clear that it will have strict analogues in a variety of political views. Thus in various versions of twentieth-century Marxism, to participate actively in bourgeois society is to have adopted a standpoint from which it is at least extremely difficult, if not impossible, correctly to see and appreciate the virtues of a classless society.

Even if one takes the most radical view (according to Kierkegaard the only genuinely religious view) as against the revived secular humanism discussed here, it does not follow that one ought to persecute in matters of religion. This part of the argument has been about the logic of belief, and the grounds for decision. Whether or not one ought to persecute (even if one goes with Pascal) will depend on the specific content of one's religious belief and perhaps on other factors; what will become impossible is only this line of argument for toleration.

---

[8] S. Kierkegaard, *Concluding Unscientific Postscript to the Philosophical Fragments* trans. H. V. Hong and E. H. Hong (Princeton: Princeton University Press, 1992).

The third argument which points in the direction of negative tolerance is the specifically political one which claims that whatever the truth about religion, the political realm has a certain kind of autonomy, and that the attempt to maintain religious unity through coercive means is bound to have negative consequences in the secular world of politics, such as civil war, which constitute a price too high to pay. This argumentative strand is independent of the other two. I might well consistently think that it is *in principle* a very good thing for all to agree in religion, that I know what the absolutely true religion is, and that I could successfully enforce its acceptance (eventually). Yet I might still also think that this is politically undesirable either (this is the early modern view) because it would be ruinous to the country since the process would require protracted civil war, or (a rather later 'liberal' view) because to enforce the uniform acceptance of the truth would require a massive apparatus of concentrated internal repression which would be undesirable on other grounds. This position already represents a retreat from what some (e.g. Kierkegaard) would think is the only genuinely religious view, because although this argument will work if I think religious unity is (merely) '*a* good thing' – i.e. one good thing among possible others – it is not so clear that it will work if I think, as a religious person ought, that religious truth is a transcendentally good thing, i.e. a thing the presence of which is so good, and the absence of which so bad, that compared with it nothing else, not even earthly peace, is of any significance at all.

Tolerance in the negative sense I have discussed up to now is quite distinct from two other concepts which seem to have a similar negative structure and which have recently been used to try to give general systematic accounts of this strand of liberalism: impartiality and neutrality. From the fact that I fail systematically to try to repress you in certain specified ways – I do not send in dragoons to burn down your churches, arrest your ministers, and disperse the congregation – it obviously does not follow that I remain impartial or neutral (or even that I am trying but failing to remain neutral or impartial) between you and your opponents. I may well think your views completely ridiculous; they may be self-evidently ridiculous. I may fund preachers from the public purse to lecture you on the error of your ways, fail to allow you to hold public office, tax you at a higher rate than others, but I may (for whatever reason) refrain from putting you in prison (it might become too expensive), or executing you (I might on independent grounds oppose capital punishment).

Relatively fancy efforts to distinguish between neutrality of outcomes (not always possible) and neutrality of reasons cited for action (possible),[9] seem pointless. Any seriously religious person will reject the very idea of neutral reasons. There are two distinct points here. First, there is the question whether there ever are any 'neutral' reasons, particularly in matters that concern one's basic world-view. Second, even if there were neutral reasons in some areas, it might be inappropriate in areas of the greatest human concern to allow oneself to be moved by reasons that are neutral. For a seriously religious person it might seem that to accept the possibility of neutrality on issues of the greatest human concern is to decide to deprive oneself of the most important human good, the possibility of leading a life which is preemptively *pervaded* by religious truth. As a secularist and atheist I would myself welcome the demise of this kind of religious view, but I do not delude myself, as many liberals seem to do, into thinking I have 'neutral' grounds on which to object to it. To say to a non-liberal that one 'ought' to look for and accept neutral reasons is just to say that one ought to be a liberal, and if that is what one thinks (and can get one's opponent to accept) then there is no need for a detour through a theory of neutral reasons. It is no surprise that one can give good liberal reasons for holding the views one holds in a liberal way (i.e. on purportedly 'neutral' grounds). An opponent who will not accept liberalism on other grounds will be likely to accept the doctrine of neutrality in any form.

It might be very nice if we could assume that we will *always*, or even very often, get agreement on neutral reasons, but there seem to me only two consistent positions here. The first is that of Habermas:[10] we have transcendentally binding grounds for *knowing* that everyone *must* be looking for a neutral standpoint, that such a standpoint is always in principle accessible to us, and that we will agree in recognising it when it is found and will all feel bound by moral arguments convincingly made from this standpoint. The second is that of Rorty:[11] agreement is where you find it; there is not more of it around than there is, and that is usually little enough. Agreement is always contingent, and its motivational force problematic. Rorty's position gives one no general grounds to assume

9 Cf. J. Waldron, especially in 'Legislation and Moral Neutrality', in his *Liberal Rights* (Cambridge: Cambridge University Press, 1993).

10 J. Habermas, *Moralbewußtsein und kommunikatives Handeln* (Frankfurt/M: Suhrkamp, 1983).

11 R. Rorty, *Contingency, Irony, and Solidarity* (Cambridge: Cambridge University Press, 1989), esp. chapter 3.

that neutral reasons will be available, no matter how hard one tries to find or invent them, and also gives no grounds for thinking that citing neutral reasons, when they are available, will have any force. Habermas' position saddles one with an archaic and inherently implausible Kantian transcendentalism. There is nothing to be gained in trying to pursue liberalism through the concept of neutrality.

By the end of the eighteenth and the beginning of the nineteenth century this notion of 'toleration' as a negative, if important, virtue which referred in the first instance to religious beliefs and practices had come to be supplanted, in the view of at least some theorists, by a conception that found positive merit in a more general state of social diversity. Thus toleration no longer came to be construed as something inherently negative, as a form of self-restraint or a failure to attack with all one's force something which it would in principle be good to be without, but which it was perhaps too costly fully to suppress. Rather it came to be thought that toleration should be connected with a positive fostering of conditions of non-conformity, heterogeneity, and diversity. Pluralism of conditions and forms of life was thought to be good in itself.

In principle there could be at least two contexts within which this positive virtue of toleration could be sensibly embedded. First one could have an Aristotelian–Leibnizian metaphysical aesthetic which committed one to the view that the best of all possible worlds would be not one of monotonous uniformity, but one with the maximal amount of diversity (produced parsimoniously from the smallest number of basic principles). It is now extremely unfashionable to think that one should draw political consequences from this kind of metaphysical view. The second context is one that is set out most clearly in the work of the late eighteenth- and early nineteenth-century German theorist Wilhelm von Humboldt. His formulation was especially influential with later liberals (through the mediation of J. S. Mill[12]), so I will now discuss the specific form in which the positive valuation of diversity, and the corresponding valuation of the fostering of such diversity, appear in his work.

Humboldt starts from a substantive philosophical view of the normative goal of human life. He calls this goal *Selbsttätigkeit*:[13] self-activity, that is, the self-initiated and self-guided development and deployment of human powers and capacities. He also makes the odd assumption, which he shares with the early Romantics, that humans are all unique in

[12] J. S. Mill, 'On Liberty', in *'On Liberty' and Other Writings*, ed. S. Collini (Cambridge: Cambridge University Press, 1989), p. 4.
[13] Humboldt, *Ideen zu einem Versuch*, pp. 22–4, 30–57.

that we all have different sets of powers and capacities, so that if we are *selbsttätig* we will become increasingly highly individuated. This allows Humboldt to speak of human autonomy, individuality, and the development of powers and capacities as if they were different sides of the same substantive human goal, of which the third, though, has a kind of special centrality and importance.

Although Humboldt speaks of *Selbsttätigkeit* as a kind of 'freedom or autonomy' it is, I think, quite important to note that his position is distinct from that of Kant and closer to that of Aristotle (or Goethe). *Selbsttätigkeit* for Humboldt is a potential property of real, empirical human powers and capacities: the power to eat, move, speak, draw, and so on. For Kant autonomy is connected with the human capacity merely to conceive of oneself in willing as standing under a maxim that could be a universal law for all rational creatures; as such the exercise of this rational willing is the be-all and end-all of the ethical life. This 'rational willing' is, however, a merely ideational activity. The relation of this capacity to the power actually to initiate real action in the human world is for Kant stunningly enigmatic in that we can never *know* anything at all about its effectiveness in the external world. In particular we can't know whether or not it is an illusion even to think we can initiate action under such a maxim. The relation of our self-conception and its associated form of 'willing' to what actually happens in the world, *including* our bodily 'actions' is an object only of a rational faith with no cognitive standing. For Humboldt this kind of 'autonomy' would be a completely inadequate specification of what could count as human freedom, or as a good human life. The emphasis on development of real human powers is something Marx takes over from Humboldt. For Marx, Kantian 'self-determination' (of the will) is not itself freedom, but at best a precondition of freedom. Full freedom requires one also to have the power to do – to realise in the external world – what one determines to make the object of volition.[14]

The political relevance of this depends on a further set of empirical assumptions about how human powers and capacities are developed and exercised. These assumptions state that despite the fact that self-activity is the normative goal and also the natural state of human being, human capacities do not generally develop of themselves, but only in response to the appropriate kind of soliciting external circumstances. Thus if I am confronted with a repeated sequence of the same external problematic

---

[14] See Marx, *Marx-Engels Werke*, vol. III, pp. 176ff., 282, 287 and also my 'Freiheit im Liberalismus und bei Marx', in *Ethische und politische Freiheit*, ed. J. Nida-Rümelin and W. Vossenkuhl (Berlin: de Gruyter, 1997), pp. 114–25.

circumstances, I will not 'naturally' experiment, but will fall into a set of routinised responses,[15] and I will generally fail to develop my powers and capacities. Uniformity and predictability in conditions of life stultify. Only if I encounter a variety of different kinds of problematic situation with which I must deal will I fully develop the widest possible variety of my human capacities. Humboldt uses this general line of argument to claim that toleration of deviance is not just a *pis aller*. Rather it is a positive contribution to the human good to foster the greatest possible diversity of forms of human behaviour and social circumstances of life, because this imposes on individuals the necessity to overcome routinised forms of reaction and develop their self-active powers. The development and exercise of such capacities, however, is the normative end for human beings.

Correlatively Humboldt draws from the above analysis the conclusion that the realm of activity of the 'state' (especially in respect of provision for the welfare of the members of the state) should be minimised. He has two reasons for this. First of all, since 'self-activity' is the normative human goal, anything that reduces that is an evil, and if I am provided with various goods and services, I need not acquire them self-actively. By the assumption cited in the last paragraph, if I *need* not acquire these goods self-actively, I will not do so, and thus will fail to attain as high a level of human excellence as would otherwise have been the case. Second, if there is central state provision of goods and services, justice will require that the goods and services provided to different individuals be roughly equal and considerations of administrative efficiency will tend towards homogeneity of provision. This is turn will tend to make the conditions of life in the society similar and predictable, and thus prevent agents in the society from being confronted with a variety which will stimulate their self-activity. Paradoxically, then, the more just such a state is, the more it prevents the realisation of the human good. The state, Humboldt argues, should therefore not be at all in the business of providing for the welfare of its members, but should be restricted to the control of violence and fraud.

There would seem to be four obvious objections to this. First, what about people who are simply incapable of being self-active, those with birth defects, etc.? Are they simply to be abandoned to private conscience and charity even if one has good reason to think these will be systematically inadequate? It seems hard completely to suppress humanitarian

[15] Marx's analysis of alienated labour in the so-called *Philosophic–Economic Manuscripts* is a natural development of this motif, see Marx, *Marx–Engels Werke* (Berlin: Dietz, 1957ff.), Ergänzungsband 1, pp. 454–63, 511ff., 539–40.

impulses and hold fast to the austere doctrine of self-activity consistently. Second, dire poverty can have the effect of making it extremely difficult, if not strictly impossible, to develop any very complex forms of self-activity. Should the state as a major locus of collective power not ensure even an absolute social minimum level of welfare in cases of need, so as to enable people to become (or become again after a period of ill health or unemployment) as self-active as it is possible for them to be? The history of modern politics in the Western democracies has shown that one can tack back and forth endlessly between these two poles without reaching any stable position: on the one hand, claims about the value of self-activity, and on the other, demands for minimal provision in certain kinds of disability ('undeserved', temporary, etc.) and perhaps even some residual moral sense of a collective responsibility for the welfare of all. Third, it may be noticed that not all state action supplants or suppresses all forms of self-activity. Humboldt himself in later years as Minister of Culture in Prussia was involved in the foundation of the reformed university system. Presumably even he thought that there were overriding good reasons for public establishment and support of an educational system and that this did not stunt but, in the long run, rather improved the chances which the individuals in Prussia had to become self-active. Finally, could there not be ways of avoiding the homogenisation through central provision which Humboldt feared? Humboldt was still thinking of a highly centralised state, but in a decentralised one with overlapping constituencies for different agencies could there not be varied and differential provision?

To take these four points seriously would, however, move one from this strict Humboldtian analysis to a position that is more open to what came later to be called 'social-democratic' ideas. One could give these ideas a superficially Humboldtian cast by claiming that to the extent to which the state must willy-nilly intervene in the economic and social sphere, it should do so in the direction of a positive discrimination in favour of the creation and maintenance of the widest possible diversity of variant circumstances of life.[16]

It is sometimes asserted that liberalism itself has no substantive conception of the human good. There are three variants of this claim: (a) liberals

---

[16] Humboldt was also extremely influential on the early Marx. In a way the young Marx and mature J. S. Mill agree on the general framework derived from Humboldt which takes individual self-development to be the end of human life, but they disagree on the social, political, and especially economic conditions under which such self-development will be possible.

simply deny that there could be such a thing as a single form of life that is best for humans, or (b) liberals are epistemically agnostic and deny that we or anyone else can *know* (or have good reason to believe) which kind of human life is best, or (c) liberals claim it is best to be politically self-denying, in that they hold that no substantive conceptions of the human good may or should legitimately play a role in legitimating political decisions (although they may appropriately function in various ways in 'private life').

To say in general that liberalism has no substantive conception of the good life is not itself prima facie terribly informative. Liberalism cannot, presumably, simply have no views about the good life at all, so how can one distinguish 'substantive' from other conceptions? The purported abstemiousness of liberalism in this respect would get whatever cognitive content it might have from a specific contrast with other views that are deemed to be committed to substantive claims.[17] It is also sometimes unclear why it should be such a great advantage in a political philosophy to have no substantive conception of the good life. Whatever might be true of later liberals, it is clear that Humboldt very explicitly rejects all three variants of this general claim and consciously draws very extensive political consequences from a highly elaborated conception of the good human life as one of self-activity. This gives Humboldt's theory a structure which is different from that of many later liberal theories. Whereas some later liberals[18] seem to suggest that that we have no clear, single criterion for evaluating the variety of human goods and ways of life, this is not the case for Humboldt. The flourishing of *Selbsttätigkeit* gives one a criterion for how far toleration should extend; a plurality of ways of life is good to the extent to which it contributes to this goal. There still remain open questions about the relation of toleration and pluralism to morality. It would seem exceedingly implausible to think that all forms of *Selbsttätigkeit* will be morally acceptable. Still, reference to *Selbsttätigkeit* may allow Humboldt to avoid embarrassment by some of the questions about the limits of toleration (for instance, toleration of intolerant attitudes) that have plagued many later, purportedly more normatively abstemious forms of liberalism.

---

[17] Marx gives the specific terms of the contrast he wishes to make between what he calls 'modern' and 'ancient' conceptions in *Grundrisse der Kritik der politischen Ökonomie* (Berlin: Dietz, 1953), pp. 387ff.

[18] I. Berlin, 'John Stuart Mill and the Ends of Life', in *Four Essays on Liberty* (Oxford: Oxford University Press, 1969), and see below, 'Conclusion'.

3. FREEDOM

The second of the four central strands of liberalism is the one that seems least specifically characteristic of liberalism as distinct from other political theories. 'Ελευθερία early became a political ideal in the slave-holding societies of ancient Greece and *libertas* was a watchword during certain periods in the Roman Republic. Nietzsche thought that it was not an accident that 'freedom' as an ideal and slavery as a widespread social institution arise at about the same time in the same place. 'Freedom', he thought, was an essentially servile ideal, as could be seen by reflecting on the fact that no one posits as an ideal worthy of motivating serious forms of sacrifice something that is an obvious property shared by everyone. Slaves and people who fear seriously that they may become slaves will rally to the banner of 'freedom'; who, apart from the patients in a emphysema ward, would rally to the banner of 'respiration for all'? Putting these thoughts aside for a moment, it is also the case that liberals are not the only ones who think freedom is a central social virtue, and have no monopoly on the claim that political authority should arise from the consent of those over whom it is exercised, and no anarchist would deny the view that on the whole voluntary arrangements are to be preferred to imposed ones.[19] Is there, then, anything distinctive about the liberal concern with freedom?

To make any progress in understanding this strand of liberalism requires a certain further discussion of the concept or concepts of freedom (or liberty).[20] I will claim that there are two levels of analysis that need to be distinguished, a formal level and a more substantive level. By calling the first level 'formal' I do not mean to denigrate it in any way, to detract either from its theoretical or its practical importance. To speak of freedom in a formal sense is just to speak of consent. A relation between two persons A and B is a free one if ideally each of the two consents to the relation. Philosophers have usually construed this to mean not that A and B *did* consent, but that they *would* (hypothetically) consent, and the consent they have given to this hypothetical is that *if* one were to ask A and B, they would affirm that the relation is a voluntary one. In chapter 1, § 9 I mentioned some of the, as it seems to me, insuperable obstacles in the way of construing political legitimacy (in the philosophical sense)

[19] See, for instance, P. Kropotkin's article for *Encyclopedia Britannica* in *The Conquest of Bread and Other Writings*, ed. M. Schatz (Cambridge: Cambridge University Press, 1996).
[20] Following I. Berlin (*Four Essays on Liberty*, p. 121), I will make no systematic distinction between freedom and liberty.

and obligation relative to the notion of consent. However this may be, I wish to assert that at a first approximation, liberalism is committed to the view that political relations which are or would be the object of such formal consent are to be preferred to those that are not, or would not be.

The notion of formal consent is too etiolated to be a plausible basis for understanding any larger fragment of politics. Consider Hobbes, who is sometimes presented as almost a proto-liberal on the grounds that he holds that all obligations arise out of agreement or consent. However, for Hobbes my consent may take the form of my agreeing to be your slave on the battlefield 'in order to avoid the present stroke of death'[21] at your hands. The circumstances of my giving that consent are irrelevant to its validity; the obligation that arises is fully binding. If even agreement to avoid the present stroke of death on the battlefield counts as 'free', then one wonders what the point of using the concept is. It is hard for us in the early twenty-first century to believe that political obligations gain any serious additional quasi-moral standing by virtue of being 'consented to' in this sense, and indeed Hobbes' own view is centred theoretically *not* on freedom or consent, but on the concept of reason. This makes him completely different from the later mainline of liberalism (and also from the strand of political thinking that originates with Rousseau).

Hobbes' own formal doctrine of 'freedom' makes no reference to 'consent' at all, but is an unremittingly naturalist and negative concept. Or rather Hobbes distinguishes two concepts of 'freedom' or 'liberty', neither one of which is of much use in political philosophy: 'freedom in the proper sense' just means non-obstruction of action. I am free in this sense just as the water in a canal is free when unimpeded. From this Hobbes distinguishes 'the freedom of the subject' which is just my ability to do whatever is permitted by the established laws and authorities in my commonwealth. This liberty is in principle no different (or greater) in the republic of Lucca than in the Ottoman Empire. An important part of Hobbes' point in giving the particular exceedingly thin account of 'freedom' he did, was precisely to undercut the possibility of appeal to the notion in the service of a rehabilitation of republicanism.[22]

During the nineteenth century the notion of formal consent (alone) as a serious origin of political, or any other kind of, obligation is subject to an ever-increasing battery of criticisms such as that by Marx. People who have little power or few resources may give formal consent to a variety

---

[21] Hobbes, *Leviathan*, p. 141.

[22] Cf. Q. Skinner, *Liberty Before Liberalism* (Cambridge: Cambridge University Press, 1998), pp. 7–11.

of agreements with those who are more powerful without it being at all reasonable to suggest that this means that the resulting arrangements are 'voluntary' in any sense of that term which has robust moral force. In the twentieth century this line of argument was given a further boost when researchers in social psychology noticed that people who have little power and see little chance of ever gaining any more power tend to develop low aspirations and that those with very low aspirations may not exhibit the symptoms of subjective discontent with what seem to the external observer to be highly coercive, oppressive, or otherwise unsatisfactory, agreements.[23] One might see this as trying to expand the idea of what counts as consent to include some features of the context within which formal consent is given. Formal consent is not *real* consent – that is, a consent that would ground a claim that the relation in question is truly voluntary and thus an instance of freedom – if it is given by impoverished people who have no reasonable alternative to 'consenting'. 'Consent or starve' is not a reasonable alternative.

Liberals vacillate on this issue. On the one hand, this basic point is so persuasive that once it has been made clearly it is extremely difficult to see how it can be evaded. On the other hand, many liberals do try. Some have tried to follow Isaiah Berlin[24] in distinguishing sharply between the content of (the concept of) freedom and the conditions under which freedom can be effectively exercised, and then claiming that politics ought to have to do only with the maximisation of freedom, not with the implementation of the conditions under which freedom can be utilised. So if I live in a society in which there is no legal or social bar to my buying some good or commodity, I have as much freedom as I ought politically to expect, even if I do not have the money to make any purchase at all, and so cannot effectively exercise that freedom.

In any case, though, this account of freedom as formal consent does not exhaust liberalism's thoughts on the subject of human freedom and the political good. To deal, however, with the more substantive level of analysis requires a slight detour which I will take once again through the work of Humboldt. Humboldt thinks that a proper understanding of politics requires one to distinguish clearly between two different questions. Only when the difference between these questions is understood, and when it is equally well understood what difference it makes to take

---

[23] See Elster on adaptive preference in *Sour Grapes*.
[24] Berlin, *Four Essays on Liberty*.

one of the two questions as having priority, can one begin to get a firm grasp on politics. The two questions are:

(a) Who rules? That is, what structures exist in society for exercising political power – how is the government organised – and who actually controls these structures and how?
(b) To which 'objects' (i.e. to which spheres of human life) ought the governmental power to extend its activity and from which ought it to be excluded?

Traditional answers to the first question include: government should be vested in an absolute monarch, or a democratic assembly elected by universal adult suffrage, or there should be a division of powers between legislature and judiciary. Answers to the second question include: government should have power over all aspects of human life, or government should care only for defence against external enemies and internal peace, or government should be prevented from establishing economic monopolies or a state religion.

Humboldt claims that traditional political theory has asked only the first of these two questions in a serious way, or at any rate has given the asking and answering of this question strict priority over the second question; he claims that in fact one should give priority to the asking and answering of the second. In so doing, he in some sense initiates one of the more important strands of the later liberal doctrine of freedom.

The connection of these two questions with the issue of freedom results from the fact that one can see each of the two questions as a gloss or interpretation of the more fundamental question: what kind of politically organised society is 'free'? The answers to each of Humboldt's two questions are really best understood as replies to the more fundamental question of freedom. Those who focus on the first question characteristically answer that that society is free which has a certain type of apparatus of government, and thus is controlled in a certain way. Thus, one version of the answer is that that society is free which governs itself, where 'governing itself' is to be understood as instantiating one or another of a relatively restricted range of preferred possible constitutional and governmental forms, such as that of the self-governing republic. Those who focus on the second question will see a free society as one in which the effective powers of government, no matter what its form or the way in which it is controlled, are as limited as possible. That society is 'freest' whose members are *most* free of the fear of being interfered with in the largest possible number of domains of their life (or alternatively in the largest number of the most important of the domains of their life[25]). There is an obvious connection between giving priority to the second question and Humboldt's more general account of freedom as self-activity. If one sees self-activity and government action as the two players in a zero-sum game, as Humboldt does, and thinks that maximal self-activity is our goal, then maximising our freedom requires minimising the sphere of possible governmental action.

One might, however, wonder whether the term 'free' is univocal in the above discussion and strongly suspect that it is being used in two different senses when it figures in the respective answers to the first and the second questions. Isaiah Berlin, in his famous Oxford inaugural lecture of 1956,[26] argued that this suspicion was very well grounded. Berlin made a highly influential distinction between two concepts or two families of concepts of liberty, a distinction that can be seen as a generalisation from the concrete political conceptions that figure in the answers to Humboldt's two distinct questions. Freedom, Berlin claims, means, on the one hand, 'self-government' as in the answer to the first question ('That society is freest that has the most fully developed structure of internal self-rule'); this Berlin calls the 'positive' conception of freedom. On the other hand, 'freedom' can also mean lack of interference from without, as in the answer to the second question ('That society is freest in which the individuals are least, externally obstructed or interfered with by government'); this Berlin calls the 'negative' conception of freedom.

It is a mistake to identify the distinction between negative and positive liberty in Berlin's sense with the mere distinction between 'freedom from' and 'freedom to'. 'Free from' has a much greater extension than 'negative liberty' in that it can designate *any* lack or absence, 'freedom from headache, doubt, care' not just absence of external obstacles to action, similarly 'free to' usually indicates either actual power or permission: 'After the operation she is free to run again' = her leg has been repaired and she is able to run, or ' You are now free to go' = you have permission to go. Berlin specifically wants to distinguish freedom from power, and to have to ask permission is not usually a sign that I am ruling myself.

The positive conception of freedom originally arose as a status term in slave-holding societies. The man who was no one's slave was positively free. The usage is then metaphorically extended to refer to the relation

---

[25] Charles Taylor, 'What's Wrong with Negative Liberty?', in *The Idea of Freedom*, ed. A. Ryan (Oxford: Oxford University Press, 1979).

[26] I. Berlin, 'Two Concepts of Liberty' in *Four Essays on Liberty*.

between societies as a whole. Thus during times of ancient Athenian military and political hegemony various of its dependencies, such as the island of Naxos, could be called 'slaves' of Athens. Athens as a whole was positively free; the dependencies were not. Finally, a society may be independent of any other society or political unit, but still fail to be internally fully self-governing, for instance, if it is ruled despotically by an indigenous tyrant. Eventually, then, the property of being an independent and internally fully self-governing society comes to be seen as being definitive of positive freedom. Negative freedom, on the other hand, views the world from the point of view of individuals in society who either are or are not obstructed, impeded, or interfered with: the individuals are free (or not). So the distinction between answers to the first and second of Humboldt's questions do not just differ in the concept of freedom involved, but also in the perspective from which the question is asked and answered, and the kind of basic entity to which the predicates 'free' or 'unfree' properly apply.

Once one has the two concepts of freedom one can, of course, extend their use from the paradigmatic case in which each arose to other cases. Thus although positive freedom is originally a property of whole (political) society one can come to apply it to an individual who is said (originally metaphorically, but the metaphor, as Nietzsche would say, 'is rubbed away and fades'[27]) to 'rule himself', where this means originally 'exercises self-control over his passions', and eventually may come to mean something like the modern idea of individual autonomy. Similarly, one could in principle speak of the negative liberty of a society as a whole: if one were speaking, for instance, of international relations in a era in which the balance of power were precarious, one could ask whether such-and-such a country was free to intervene in this way in the affairs of another country (e.g. by invading). This would mean whether this course of action was or was not blocked or obstructed. To be sure the notion of 'external obstruction' in this case would be a sophisticated one. In some cases there might be a huge impeding geographic feature or human construction like the Maginot Line or the Great Wall of China, but usually the 'obstacle' would be the threat of reprisal by some other country. Still the situation would not be strikingly different from the case of the individual confronting a government. When people said that citizens in certain countries were not free to practise religions, the 'obstacle' to freedom there, too, was not a wall or physical shackle, but

---

[27] Nietzsche, 'Über Wahrheit und Lüge in einem außermoralischen Sinne', in *Kritische Gesamtausgabe*, vol. I, pp. 880–1.

the threat that the government would punish religious activities with loss of job, reduction of pay, withdrawal of passport, and so on. The notion of an 'obstacle' is a flexible one that needs interpretation, but that is true equally in the case of individuals confronted by governmental obstacles and societies encountering obstacles in international politics.

To be fully clear, then, Berlin needs one to make a four-fold distinction, not just a two-fold one, between: (1) positive concepts of the liberty of a society, (2) positive concepts of the liberty of an individual, (3) negative concepts of the liberty of a society and (4) negative concepts of the liberty of an individual. The third of these kinds of concepts, although of great importance in assessing actual situations in international politics, has not played much of a role in liberal political philosophy, but the remaining three are an illuminating apparatus for understanding retrospectively the intentions and history of liberalism.

To return to the two Humboldtian questions which are the origin of Berlin's distinction, although it might be to some extent an exaggeration, it is nevertheless a theoretically enlightening exaggeration to see the confrontation between two views about which of Humboldt's two questions has priority (and thus correlatively about how freedom is properly to be understood) as instantiated in the notional conflict between Jacobins and liberals.[28]

Jacobins give Humboldt's first question (and the positive conception of the liberty of the society as a whole) strict priority. There is, however, a weaker and a stronger Jacobin position. For the Jacobins, if one answered the first of the two questions correctly and implemented that answer fully, there was no need to worry about the answer to the second question. This is the weaker position. The 'right' answer to the first question, for the Jacobins, was that the best political society was a self-governing republic with a very high level of political participation on the part of the citizens. And after all, they would argue, if one really did have such a fully free republic in which the mechanisms of self-government operated without the hindrance or distortion of private or sectional interest, why would one have to worry about how far the power of such an apparatus could reach? Such an apparatus would by definition be not just open to public observation and control, but itself the very instrument of public power. What motive would anyone have for opposing

---

[28] 'Jacobin' and 'liberal' are here Weberian ideal types (cf. Weber, 'Die "Objektivität sozialwissenschaftlicher und sozialpolitischer Erkenntnis', in *Gesammelte Aufsätze zur Wissenschaftslehre* (Tübingen: Mohr, 1973), pp. 190–214). The doctrine of ideal types is, I think, one of Weber's most notable contributions to the study of the history of political thought.

the power of a fully free self-governing political community, apart from private interest or the desire to evade the scrutiny of vicious, corrupt, or immoral actions that would not bear the light of day? To be sure, the mechanism might be sound, but the particular people in positions of authority might be morally corrupt. This would be a case of moral failing on the part of particular human individuals. One could prevent it by ensuring that the whole life of all members of the society was conducted in conditions of the greatest possible publicity and thus always open to scrutiny. Since one's moral character is something that will eventually reveal itself clearly in such circumstance, one would be able easily to see which citizens were morally upright, and thus appropriate candidates for political power and authority, and which were weak or corrupt. In addition, if the mechanism *was* corrupt so that it was appropriate for citizens to be afraid of it, surely the right remedy was the robust, political one of changing the structure of power so as to heal it, rather than the defeatist one of restricting the public power.

If, then, the mechanism is in order (and appropriately staffed with morally upright, competent, and reliable persons), one has no reason to limit its extent, and if it is not in order, the appropriate remedy is a change of the structure (or the incumbents), that is, giving a correct answer to the first question and implementing this answer properly. This implies making the republic *more* truly self-governing and involving more of the population in the active exercise of their political powers, not a limitation of the powers of the government. What is truly important is setting up and maintaining the correct mechanism of government (and perhaps ensuring the personal morality of the incumbents); the answer to the first question always trumps the second. The stronger Jacobin position adds to the above the suspicion that even suggesting limitations to state power must be a sign that those making such a suggestion are guilty of *incivisme*: if they had nothing to hide and were morally upright, why would they oppose the public power of the republic?

The archetypal liberal position is the mirror image of this. If one starts from the second question and gives the correct answer to it, one will restrict state power so that the individuals in the society are as free – as little interfered with by the state – as possible, then it really will not matter who wields the merely residual minimal powers of the state or how they are organised.

Jacobins and liberals seem to agree at one level in that they both seem to think that freedom is the basic or the most important virtue of a form of political organisation. This is by no means a trivial thing to agree on. Many theorists would have rejected it. No ancient thinker would have agreed with this view, and presumably every Christian, Jewish, or Muslim thinker holds that being god-fearing is more important than being free. Similarly Rawls thinks that justice (not freedom) is the basic virtue of a society,[29] Margalit the absence of systematic forms of humiliation,[30] and Shklar/Rorty[31] the avoidance of cruelty. Although, however, liberals and Jacobins seem to agree on the centrality of freedom, the consensus is merely a verbal one and they actually mean very different things, in two slightly different dimensions, by calling a society 'free'. For the Jacobins, the society or political system as a whole is free if it rules, regulates, and governs itself. Individuals can be called free in one or both of two senses: (a) derivatively if they participate fully in the self-governance of the society, that is, if they lead an active politically involved life, or (b) if they 'rule themselves' in a psychological and moral sense, that is, if they control their passions, and subject them fully and correctly to the guidance of reason.[32] For liberals a society is free by virtue of being composed of free individuals, and the individuals are (negatively) free by virtue of being maximally unimpeded or unhindered by external obstacles in their action placed in their path by the government, or more generally if there is as little governmental intervention in the lives of the individual citizens as possible.

Constant was the early liberal theorist who gave this rather abstract oppositional scheme both conceptual sharpness and some historical and sociological content. Jacobinism, Constant argued, was a historical anachronism. In the ancient world of small, belligerent, (potentially) directly self-governing cities, the pleasures of participation in politics were keen and eagerly sought after. Given that systematic forms of commercial activity were relatively undeveloped and marginal, the sphere of private consumption was extremely restricted compared with modern times, and thus the pleasures of private life were modest. On the whole, what people really cared about under those circumstances was full, active

[29] J. Rawls, *A Theory of Justice* (Cambridge, Mass.: Harvard University Press, 1971).
[30] A. Margalit, *The Decent Society* (Cambridge, Mass.: Harvard University Press, 1996).
[31] J. Shklar, *Ordinary Vices* (Cambridge, Mass.: Harvard University Press, 1984), pp. 7–44; Rorty, *Contingency, Irony, and Solidarity*, p. 74.
[32] These two senses are each variants on the 'positive' concept of freedom for individuals. In other works I have called them 'positive freedom of the individual in an outward-looking sense' – freedom as participation in the self-governance of society – and 'positive freedom of the individual in an inward-looking sense' – psychological self-control and moral autonomy. Cf. my 'Freedom as an Ideal', in *Proceedings of the Aristotelian Society*, Supplementary volume LXIX (1995), pp. 87–100, 'Auffassungen der Freiheit', in *Zeitschrift für philosophische Forschung* (1995), pp. 1–14, and 'Freiheit im Liberalismus und bei Marx'.

participation in politics. In such a world the 'liberty of the ancients' – the ability to participate in the personal exercise of extensive public power in ancient direct democracies – was rightly prized above all else, and people were willing to accept that in such a society they would have no inviolable private sphere.

The modern world has seen a drastic reversal of this order of priorities. In a commercial society private life is much more highly developed, and because modern societies are also geographically larger and more populous than ancient societies were, most people are of necessity excluded from direct, palpable exercise of political power. For all but a few people at the absolute centres of power, the political sphere in the modern world is not the realm of the keenest and most intense pleasures and final self-definition, but a far-away shadowy world which one can only hope to influence in a highly indirect way. In the modern world people want a peaceful enjoyment of the varied pleasures of private life and time to get on with their commercial transactions, and are less willing to brook infringement of these either in the name of quasi-compulsory civic activities (which must by the nature of the case be personally less than fully satisfactory because their relation to real power is so highly mediated) or by interference from central authorities. This immunity of the private sphere *from* politics is the characteristic 'freedom of moderns'. The modern invention of representative government with built-in protections against excessive interference of that government in the private sphere corresponds to the modern temperament, giving individuals *some* control over government (albeit an indirect one through election of representatives) and yet defending them against either the need for strenuous engagement or fear of excessive intervention. The Jacobins were abstract doctrinaires (and eventually failed ones) because they attempted to realise under modern conditions a form of freedom which was appropriate only in the conditions that prevailed in antiquity, and which modern people did not want.

It would be incorrect simply to identify Constant's distinction between the 'liberty of the ancients' and the 'liberty of the moderns' with Berlin's positive and negative liberty. Berlin's notion of positive liberty is intended to be general and to cover a wide range of forms of self-governance, including, but not restricted to, the specific form of direct democracy which is Constant's ideal 'freedom of the ancients'. Similarly freedom from governmental interference (Berlin's negative liberty) is a central component of 'the freedom of the moderns', but modern freedom also comprises the particular kind of indirect political control which Constant sees embodied in representative institutions. Still, if one wanted a one-sentence summary, it would not be incorrect to say that a certain kind of positive liberty is the core of the freedom of the ancients, while the negative freedom of the individual has special salience in the liberty of the moderns.

The liberal gives priority to Berlin's negative liberty of the individual, that is, to the 'modern' freedom of the individual *from* obstacles and impediments to action and from interference. What, however, counts as an obstacle and what counts as interference? In fact liberals interpret 'absence of interference' as absence of interference *by the government*. If the issue is really how free I am in society, or how free I am in a politically relevant sense, then even if the basic sense of 'freedom' is the negative one, are there not *other* possible sources of interference, in addition to the government, that ought to be recognised? There could be natural obstacles to my action: the finitude of my life, for instance, might prevent me from realising certain very long-term projects, or interference could have its source in other individuals or non-governmental groups. Why does only governmental interference count? Perhaps the government could interfere in individuals' lives in such a way as to make it safe from intervention by *other people*, as when the police (in some other countries) shoot into a crowd to prevent a lynching or riot. Similarly, why should it not be construed as an increase in my liberty if the government intervenes to regulate the massive intereference in my life that is effected by large corporations or other economic agents? Why does this not count as an increase in the freedom of the society?

The reason, Berlin argues, is that this is supposed to be a political doctrine, and politics is about what people consciously and deliberately do to each other, especially through the employment of formal collective social power, and not about natural obstacles to action or other forms of human obstruction. Berlin, in common with the main line of liberal thought, wishes to construe the possible 'obstacles' to negative freedom as narrowly as possible. This response seems to me to arise out of a deep misapprehension about political and social life.

Why assume that an obstacle is a restriction of human negative freedom only if it results from a conscious deliberate human action? Why not rather think that anything that is the kind of thing that could be *changed* by human action can count as a possible relevant obstruction? To be sure, the natural limitation of the human life span is perhaps not a limitation to politically significant freedom for as long as and to the extent to which it is not subject to human control. If one is living in a world in which most people cannot expect to live beyond seventy, and there is no *reliable* way of increasing their chances of reaching seventy-five, then perhaps the limit of the 'natural' human life span to seventy is not a politically relevant restriction of human freedom. Once medical and social factors make it possible, however, to prolong the 'natural human life span' (as it has always been possible to curtail it through murder), then it becomes a possible object of human deliberation and political decision. If most people get a drug that allows them to live to the age of ninety, no one could say that failing to give that drug to me is not in some sense a restriction of my 'negative liberty' even if my death at seventy-one is a result of natural causes, and even if my failure to get the drug does not result from a formal decision. If such things as the natural limitation of the human life span do not generally count as obstacles, the reason is not that they do not result from deliberate human action, but rather that we assume that they could not be changed by any action we could undertake. They are not relevant to the extent to which that claim is true. One can extend this analysis to the politics of developing (or failing to develop) new technologies.

A further tack one could take to defend the narrow construal of 'obstacle' is to distinguish sharply between 'doing' something and simply allowing it to happen – thus, in the case cited above, between 'withholding' the drug from me, and merely letting me die for want of it. The distinction between doing something and simply allowing it to happen is sometimes useful or important, but it is not so in this case. As a general rule one must accept that anything that *can* or *could* become an object of political decision will become an object of discussion because it is an object of possible action. That something is radically beyond our control is *no longer* the fall-back assumption, but must be specifically demonstrated, or at any rate it is always an open possibility that it will have to be demonstrated. Nothing is sacred, beyond bounds, off limits, 'natural' (in a sense that excludes possible human control and decision). That this is the case is a tremendously important and often remarked property of fully modern societies. Marx,[33] Max Weber,[34] and Heidegger[35] – the political left, centre, and right – all agree on this as a correct diagnosis of our contemporary world. Certain residually religious, politically conservative,

---

[33] This strand in Marx's work is especially illuminatingly discussed in M. Berman, *All that is Solid Melts into Air* (New York: Simon & Schuster, 1982), esp. chapter II.

[34] The doctrine of the *Entzauberung* of the whole natural universe was, originally, Weber claims, a Puritan motif, which then is itself gradually secularized. *Wirtschaft und Gesellschaft*, pp. 307–8 and *Gesammelte Aufsätze zur Religionssoziologie* (Tübingen: Mohr, 1920), pp. 94–5.

[35] M. Heidegger, 'Die Zeit des Weltbildes', in *Holzwege* (Frankfurt/M: Klostermann, 1950), pp. 69–105.

or ecologically minded thinkers have pointed out what they take to be highly undesirable consequences of this widespread attitude, the attitude that anything that can be discussed will be discussed, and reasons will have to be given for a decision to act *or not to act*. In any case, no one, as far as I can see, has any idea how one could even begin to try to do away with this attitude without amounts of coercion and social regression that few in Western Europe would find acceptable. As long as this attitude persists as a widely shared one, it makes no sense *in general* to focus on 'obstacles' alone in the narrow sense envisaged by Berlin.

Liberals have had the right intuition when they have thought that it was necessary for them, if they were to maintain the distinctiveness of their position, to hold as firmly as possible to a distinction between freedom and the conditions under which freedom can be effectively used or between freedom and empowerment. This is one of the main differences between Marxism and liberalism, despite their common concern with the Humboldtian idea of self-development. Marxism thinks it ridiculous to discuss freedom except relative to power. I am free must finally mean 'I am able to ...', and I may fail to be able to ... either because of obstacles or because of lack of power. Structurally these two possibilities look parallel. The only real reason to be interested in possible 'obstacles to action' is that one thinks it is better to have *more* possible courses of action open rather than fewer. How many courses of action are open depends, however, not merely on the presence or absence of obstacles, but on the conjunction of the power one has and the obstacles that stand in one's way. I can fail to be free to arrive at a certain point in space, for example, a certain mountain top, either because I am prevented by an 'obstacle' or because I lack strength and energy. Furthermore, in the larger context what counts as an 'obstacle' is in most cases not an independently specified magnitude, but is relative to my state of power. If I were stronger, what is now an obstacle to me, for instance, a particular expanse of rock-face, would not be a hindrance. If, however, the existence of obstacles counts as a limitation on freedom, why not absence of power? Liberals shy away from this whole idea. Once one begins to see that what is important is control/power, not obstacles, forms of liberal epistemic, ethical, and political abstemiousness become increasingly difficult to maintain. It becomes possible to see the phenomenon which liberals have great difficulty looking at firmly: that of real conflict of interest (and real difference in power) that cannot be reasoned away, on which there may be no possibility of compromise or agreement, and relative to which there is no neutral standpoint.[36]

4. INDIVIDUALISM

The third strand of liberalism I wish to discuss is individualism. Although many nineteenth-century liberals were 'methodological individualists' or even 'ontological individualists',[37] it is not really central to the liberal project to assume either that individuals can exist independent of society or that all forms of knowledge about society are reducible in some sense to claims about individuals.[38] What is important for liberalism are two forms of individualism: a certain two-stage value-individualism, and a certain teleological individualism.

To start with the first of these, liberalism is committed to a certain two-stage view about how human valuation and its objects are to be understood. At the first stage one asks the question: what are the final objects of valuation in politics, that is, what kind of entities are to be judged as in the first instance or directly valuable in a way that should impinge on political decisions? The liberal answer to this is: the final bearers of politically relevant value are in each case human individuals, and in some sense the goal of any human society must be the well-being of individuals. This means that, for instance, there are no structural properties of societies as a whole which are valuable in themselves and apart from their contribution to the well-being of the individual members of the society, and *a fortiori* there are no non-individual, transcendental values (such as that the society as a whole has the property of being god-fearing, or 'organic') which have standing as goals for political action (or perhaps as goals for those forms of political action that require or imply coercion). Second, liberals hold that individuals are not only the objects of valuation, but also in a very deep sense the only potential subjects of valuation. Whatever is valuable is valuable because some individual or other values it. Only the acts of valuation performed by individuals are, finally, to count politically. That is, when liberals say that in politics in the final analysis 'value' must be understood in a way which refers it essentially to individuals, they mean both that a society has what value it has

---

[36] See my 'Freedom as an Ideal'.

[37] For an analysis of the varieties of 'individualism' See S. Lukes, *Individualism* (Oxford: Blackwell, 1973); cf. also L. Dumont, *Homo Hierarchicus: The Caste System and its Implications* (Chicago: University of Chicago Press, 1970).

[38] See J. Durkheim 'L'individualisme et les intellectuels', in *Revue bleue* 10, 1898.

because the individuals in it have certain properties – these individuals are the final objects of valuation – and that the final judgement of value must be one which uses standards that human individuals could and would use for evaluating the good: human individuals and their possible standards of the good, and not non-individual, metaphysical entities like God or History or Reason, or Society, are the subjects whose valuing is relevant.

The second of the above principles might seem to allow the possibility of reintroducing some of the purported objects of value apparently excluded by the first principle, but allowing them to reappear in a slightly different guise. Liberals have, I think, been rather split on this issue. On the one hand, one could argue as follows: structural features of society as a whole or transcendental states, such as the society 'being in a state of grace', *can* be admitted as politically relevant to the extent to which they are the objects of valuation by individual members of the society. If individuals (positively) value these items or features, then to the extent to which they exist, they contribute to the well-being of individuals. God gets a look-in as a possible value *because* (and *only* because and to the extent to which) he is loved and valued by individual humans. To the extent to which he *is* thus valued, however, it could be argued, he has just the same unobjectionable value-status as tea, warm baths, or string quartets if I appreciate them.

On the other hand, liberals have pointed out that a God whose value consists in being prized by human individuals is not what most religious believers, with the exception of some exotic medieval mystics like Meister Eckhardt, have ever meant by 'God'. God cannot really reappear in the guise of the object of a subjective individual preference because if he can wear this habit comfortably, he was not much of a God to begin with, and if he is really a full-blooded God, the 'guise' is deceptive camouflage which will allow religious fanaticism to infiltrate the public realm of politics in a way that liberalism finds objectionable. This suggests that liberal individualism should disallow at least some non-individual 'value-objects' on the grounds that individuals who propose them as objections of valuation are either confused or duplicitous.

To say that the valuation is conducted from the value-standpoint of 'human individuals' in some further unspecified sense may be useful in helping us keep a grip on the Enlightenment project of a fully this-worldly politics, but one of the most basic facts we know about human individuals is that they *differ* in the way they value things. From the fact that I know that the valuation must be conducted from the possible standpoint of

human individuals (not of God or Reason), it does not follow that I
know *whose* standpoint to adopt: that of Mother Theresa, Field-Marshal
Montgomery, Sulpicia, Virgina Woolf, or the lady who sells me scones
in the local bakery at 7 o'clock each morning.

The general claim, then, that valuation should be from the point of
view of human individuals is usually supplemented by the further claim
that judgements about what is good for me should be judgements made
from my point of view, using standards that I do or could accept, and that
judgements about political arrangements and actions should be made
from the point of view of those either directly or indirectly concerned.[39]
To put it slightly differently, the 'well-being' of the individuals is what
they themselves in the final analysis judge or recognise (or could judge
or recognise) to constitute their own well-being, even if what they finally
see as their well-being is something very peculiar indeed.

'Judge or recognise in the final analysis' here must, unfortunately, be
construed in a highly theoretical way. The final judgement, then, about
my own well-being cannot be identified with anything I happen to *say* in
random circumstances, and the final judgement of whether a society is
in a good state cannot be identified with a state in which the individuals
who constitute the society all unanimously *say* that they are in a good
state. We must at least allow for the possibility that any such individual
judgement is distorted by ignorance, misinformation, error, momentary
distracting passions, etc. It seems no more than reasonable, then, to assume that there must at least be a built-in filtering mechanism which
will allow one to correct for such distortions. I should not be held to
my spontaneous judgement that a certain drug is valuable if that judgement is made in ignorance of very harmful side-effects which happen
not yet to have revealed themselves. The more one reflects, however, the
more extensive and complex the filtering mechanisms will be likely to
get,[40] and the more complex the apparatus gets, the more difficult it is
reliably to predict the outcome of its operations. I know what you now
say you value, but how can I be sure I know what you *would* say you
value, if you were to be asked about that *after* the filtering mechanism
had rendered some of your most deeply held but erroneous beliefs in-
operative? The more complex the filtering process, the more likely its

---

[39] It is by no means obvious who is concerned in every action. One strand of liberalism (J. S.
Mill) construes 'concern' here in a highly concrete way. I am not 'concerned' in your religious
activities, if it is merely the *thought* of what you are doing that bothers me. Cf. R. P. Wolff, *The Poverty
of Liberalism* (Boston: Beacon Press, 1968).

[40] I discuss this issue further in *The Idea of a Critical Theory* (Cambridge: Cambridge University Press,
1981).

operation will take one away from anything the agents in question would spontaneously assert about their own state.

'I am the final judge of what I value' means, then, not 'What I say about my own valuation at any given time is to be taken as canonical' but 'What I *would* say about valuation is canonical.' 'Would say', though, *under what circumstances?* What I would say, if I were given this-or-that bit of information? What I would say if I were given a full course of reeducation? What I would say if I were living in a society in which there was self-evidently enough food for all? What I would say if I were living in a region subject to drought? What I would say if I had not grown up in a society in which certain highly dubious beliefs are taken for granted by almost everyone? How this counterfactual is formulated concretely and how its potential truth value is evaluated is of the greatest political consequence. Under what circumstances is my judgement that I am in a good state (or a bad state) definitive? How do I *now* know what I *would* judge in radically modified circumstances? The welfare, then, of the individuals (and thus the good state of the society as a whole) is not taken to consist in their satisfying some externally applied standard (such as having a certain daily caloric intake, a certain kind of shelter, a certain level of medical services, etc.) but consists in the satisfaction of some standard that they themselves accept. People are, however, often not fully aware of the valuations they make or the standards they use. In fact they may not use formal standards or criteria at all, and may be inconsistent. Any claim that I am using the standards 'you (singular or plural)' do, would, or could use is a highly theoretical claim. How do I know how to winkle out inconsistencies in your views? How do I know that in determining what standards you use I am not also *changing* them? This is a question that has (rightly) come to obsess anthropologists. Liberalism is deeply committed to what is usually called 'anti-paternalism': the view that the agents must themselves be the final judges of what is good for them.

The forms of individualism I have described up to now have been rather abstract conditions on the way valuation is to be understood and conducted; that is, it could be thought, they have not referred to any concrete social ideal, a teleological conception of a form of society to which we should aspire. Such a teleological ideal is, however, also an important part of liberalism, although the question of how such a concrete ideal is compatible with the claims to neutrality which some forms of liberalism make, is unresolved. Each agent has a set of standards or criteria of what is good (even if these are merely tacit and implicit in action), but ideally, so the liberal argues, no individual should simply accept such standards and criteria from the surrounding environment, taking them over wholesale and unexamined from others. Rather, individuals should have an experimental attitude towards the good and towards their own lives, should themselves test claims about what is good, and verify them for themselves. In the best case they should value things by standards which they themselves actively develop. A good life, then, is a life lived according to a standard or conception which the individual in question has gradually invented or created by and for himself or herself, and liberals share the view derived from Romanticism that such a life can be expected to differ at least in some significant details from one individual to the next.

Two components of this general ideal can be distinguished. The first is a principle of 'autopsy' or 'pregustation'. This principle prescribes that I do not simply think and act as most other people in my society think and act, but that I use my own faculties to evaluate claims about what counts as a good life, and I act on those claims only when I have convinced myself through my own efforts of their plausibility. This is a kind of directive, addressed to individuals about how they should live. The second is a principle of uniqueness, that if I adopt the principle of 'autopsy' and act only on claims about the good it leads me to endorse, my life will be that of a unique individual. This does not seem to be best construed as an injunction or directive. I am not enjoined to strive to be unique; that would in any case be a recipe for silliness. Rather, the second principle is a prediction of what will happen, if everyone acts on the principle of autopsy, coupled with a judgement that a society populated by unique individuals would be a good and admirable one.

As part of a personal ideal of life, the first of these two components seems excessively demanding to be prescribed to everyone. Perhaps I am by nature sufficiently well suited to life in my society that I can relax and enjoy the comforts it offers to one of my disposition and talents without reflecting too much on whether this life is really good. It is also important to keep in mind that a human life is a finite, irreversible, unique process, characterised by a very high degree of social and psychological hysteresis, so there are limits to the extent to which I can try out forms of life in order to determine whether or not they are good. Since I cannot always cross out earlier attempts completely and start again from scratch, this restricts the amount of real experimentalism I can engage in: I cannot necessarily try out myself the life of a professional boxer and then expect to be in a position to try out in the same way the life of a professional violinist, if my fingers have been broken too often during my life as a boxer.

As far as the second component is concerned, one should in any case not put too much emphasis on 'uniqueness'. In an ontological sense every human being is automatically unique because uniquely instantiated by spatio-temporal position, so the uniqueness in question must be some kind of value-uniqueness.[41] 'Uniqueness' and 'comparability' form what is sometimes called a pair of concepts of reflection. That is, to say that X is unique means: unique along some dimension, for example, capable of hitting a higher note than any other singer, or of shifting more tonnage of coal per day than anyone else. In all these cases, to say that X is unique means that X can very well be compared to any given Y (and will be found to be superior).

Although these reflections may require us to be more realistic about the ideal of individuality than some have been in the past, they do not in any sense discredit it as a personal aspiration. Above (on pp. 83–4) I mentioned the difficulty some liberals might have in deciding whether or not they are committed to a substantive conception of the good human life. One might still think that there is some tension between some of the basic properties of this particular highly specific ideal of human life and the possibilities of fostering such an ideal through political action. That is, there might be thought to be some difficulty about the project of setting out to help others discover their own uniqueness, but there is no paradox about how one encourages people to think of themselves as individuals. One gives each individual a distinct name or number, a national identity card or passport, and a national insurance account, forces each individual to keep separate financial accounts and to fill out a separate income tax form each year, organises games in school pitting individuals against each other, and rewarding performance differentially, and so forth.[42] Liberals might admit that there are, of course, other values that in some circumstances are more important for politics than individualism. For instance, self-preservation might be an independent value or ideal distinct from, and prior to, individualism. Working out an original mode of life may be a luxury for those literally starving to death. Many liberals have been very clear in accepting this point, admitting that liberalism was not a universal political philosophy, but one that could become applicable only under certain highly favourable historical circumstances in which basic problems of survival and security were

---

[41] The best discussion known to me of uniqueness and its relation to valuation is still H. Rickert, *Die Grenzen der naturwissenschaftlichen Begriffsbildung* (Tübingen: Mohr, 1921) (4th edn). Cf. also Marx, *Marx-Engels Werke*, vol. III, pp. 423–6.

[42] Foucault, *Surveiller et punir*.

already resolved.[43] Similar remarks could well be made about the liberal virtue of toleration. This is a reasonable virtue to practise in societies that are themselves already relatively tolerant, but is suicidal in many others. This would mean that liberalism would not be a free-standing form of thinking about politics, but one that needed to be embedded in a more encompassing form of reflection.

5. LIMITED, UNLIMITED, AND DISCRETIONARY POWER

The fourth and final strand in historical liberalism which I wish to distinguish is the suspicion of, and opposition to, absolute or discretionary power. I have already mentioned Humboldt's arguments for restricting the power of the state, arguments that derive from his substantive conception of the human good, but a complementary motivation arises from some very deeply rooted human psychological responses to the phenomena of power and of powerlessness. There are four slightly different aspects of this dimension of power to which liberals could object. First, one could think that as a general rule what people can do, they eventually will do, and that unlimited power is likely to contribute to the moral corruption of those who wield it. Second, one may fear that if power is too great or too concentrated relative to the powers of the human individuals who are subjected to it, those individuals will feel overwhelmed or intimidated. This may be thought to be undesirable for various reasons. For instance, one might think that full and relatively uninhibited political participation by all the members of a society, especially in such functions as deliberation, was a public good, and one might also think that too much concentrated power could have the effect of inhibiting many people from such participation. Excessive concentration of power could then be thought to have a generally distorting effect on human life.

Third, one might worry that unpredictability in the exercise of power was inherently irrational and to be avoided. If power is exercised in a way that is unpredictable, this may be experienced as a source of anxiety by agents who wish to exert control over their future. Fourth, many agents find it more repugnant to feel themselves 'in the power' of another human individual than to be subject to an equivalent amount of power exercised over them by some natural constellation of forces. Thus, following Rousseau, we can contrast a case in which a snowstorm

[43] See Mill, 'On Liberty', pp. 13f.

confines me to the house and the case in which another person locks me in. Rousseau claims that although the 'objective' degree of constraint may be the same in both cases, in the second case my reaction will be likely to have a quality and intensity it will lack in the first case.[44]

The modern state wielding significant powers of coercion and armed with a moral authority it derives from its claim to legitimacy is a very daunting presence in the lives of modern individuals. That it can success-fully claim this authority increases the state's power because individuals who accept the state's moral authority will find it more difficult to resist or evade its demands. Liberalism is not a simple reaction against the royal absolutism of the early modern period – historically it does not get started as a movement until after the heyday of such royal absolutism (although liberals did oppose belated versions of royal absolutism they encountered). As long, in fact, as the major source of oppression was an absolutist king, it was possible to believe that the problem lay either with the personal properties of the incumbent – the next one might be better and one should devote time to prayer for a good succession on the one hand, and the proper education of royal princes on the other – or with the form of government, so that if the monarchy was replaced by a republican constitution all would be well. Liberalism only comes into its own when people are forced to realise that a republic which takes over the powers of an absolutist state can be just as oppressive as a monarch.[45] The Committee of Public Safety can be as bad as any Louis. Thus the trouble does not lie in the personnel or the form of government, but in the unlimited power and authority of the ruling office.

Liberals have tried in two further ways to limit the excessive accu-mulation of political power. On the level of the political system, they have tended in the first place to favour the promulgation of a *written* con-stitution, thinking this one especially important restraint on arbitrary exercise of power. In fact, the original 'liberal' parties were essentially parties devoted to demanding that traditional kings bind themselves to obey written constitutions. A written constitution by itself without the appropriate framework of institutions, practices, and social habits is not only no panacea, but a dead letter. The Constitution of the old Soviet Union was a highly edifying document, but it was a work of the imag-ination, a kind of political science fiction, and the fact that the written constitution of ex-Yugoslavia explicitly gave the constituent Republics

---

[44] J. J. Rousseau, *Emile ou de l'éducation* (Paris: Garnier, 1964), esp. Book IV.
[45] B. Constant, 'De la liberté des anciens comparée à celle des modernes' in *De la liberté chez les modernes*, ed. M. Gauchet (Paris: Hachette, 1980), pp. 502–4.

the right of secession was, when the time came, no obstacle at all to the civil wars that accompanied the attempt to invoke this right. This does not mean that a written constitution *together with* the appropriate set of institutional powers and habits of acting is of no value whatever as a check to arbitrary rule.

Liberals have also tended to support particular kinds of written constitutional arrangements, for instance, provisions for the institutionalisation of the separation of powers, and the so-called system of checks and balances. On the level of society they have tried to foster and encourage the development of so-called 'intermediary institutions';[46] these are institutions, such as clubs, fraternal organisations, and voluntary associations of all kinds, that stand between the individual citizen and the state-structure, and can mobilise opinion and perhaps even some power to counterbalance and thus limit the power of the state.

Some self-described liberals[47] have gone beyond constitutionalism and tried to revive the old conception of a *Rechtsstaat* as a way of limiting the unpredictability of political power. The *Rechtsstaat* is a more extensive ideal than that of constitutionalism. A constitution is generally a rather limited document which fixes the basic form of governmental operations and enunciates certain general principles to which these operations are to conform, but which does not actually contain particular directives for everyday legislation or administration. It leaves open large areas that could potentially be regulated by specific legislation or administrative decree; the details are to be filled in by people on the ground at any given time. Thus the constitution may specify that citizens may be taxed only by a representative assembly of a certain kind that makes decisions in a certain way, but it will not itself set the actual rate of taxation, the mode of collection, the specific penalties for non-payment, etc. The idea of the *Rechtsstaat* goes beyond this in that it envisages not just a state with a general constitutional framework, but a state in which general laws, not individual humans, are supreme *throughout*.

Such a state certainly does make the exercise of power less unpredictable than it would be in an an absolute despotism in which the prince is *legibus solutus* (above the laws). In one sense it can also be said

---

[46] The recently fashionable term 'civil society' is mostly a confusion, but to the extent that it has some use, it is a new word to refer to such a sphere of intermediary institutions.

[47] To be sure, many of these were relatively right-wing liberals like Fr. Hayek, cf. his *The Constitution of Liberty* (University of Chicago Press, 1960), pp. 193ff.

to limit absolute power, because each particular instance of exercise of power in such a system is dependent on specific authorisation by a formally correct general law. Nevertheless, the legal system might be so repressive that the fact that it was philosophically not 'absolute' seemed Pickwickian. Its power might still be in human terms excessive, even if not strictly absolute. In more general terms whether or not it can be the embodiment of liberal principles depends on the specific *nature* of the legal and political system in question. One could have a *Rechtsstaat* which enforced in a completely fair-minded, general, and non-idiosyncratic way a prohibition on all public religious activities, miscegenation, consumption of alcohol, wearing buttons on one's coat, or listening to music performed by more than one instrument at a time. There is nothing in the idea of a *Rechtsstaat* which makes it more likely than not that it will be to any particular degree tolerant or concerned with individualism or with any freedom its members have (apart from the freedom to do what the law demands or allows). That no one in a *Rechtsstaat* will have a motivation to impose an excessively repressive regime on everyone equally, is like the parallel arguments in Rousseau that were thought by liberals to lead to Jacobin tyranny,[48] and thus it is not a line one would expect liberals to be terribly keen to pursue.

That a political association is a *Rechtsstaat* does not in itself make it liberal. Furthermore, to attempt in a thoroughgoing and comprehensive way to oppose a discretionary power which is to some extent unpredictable is not a coherent project, because such discretionary power is of the essence of politics. First of all, one might wonder whether it is in principle ever possible to make the exercise of power completely predictable by setting down absolutely unambiguous guidelines for its use which require and allow no interpretation. Politics sometimes has to do with the application of general principles to particular cases, but, as Kant and others have emphasised, one cannot give rules for subsuming individual cases under general principles.[49] It is a property of general guidelines, rules, and laws that they do not interpret themselves and apply themselves automatically to individual situations. They need to be applied and this requires a constructive activity on the part of the person doing the application. Finally, one must simply exercise one's faculty of judgement.

[48] See above, chapter 2, § 3.
[49] What Kant calls *Urteilskraft* and *Mutterwitz (Kritik der reinen Vernunft,* ed. R. Schmidt, Hamburg: Meiner, 1956, B 171–4).

In addition, it is also the case that politics is in part about dealing with the unexpected, and one of the points of having public officials and a government at all is to allow them to respond quickly and flexibly to urgent matters that have not been anticipated. Sometimes such decisions are practically irreversible – it may be relatively easy to sell the railways off, but once you have done that, given the financial realities of the contemporary world, it becomes extremely unlikely that any future government will be able[50] to renationalise them. Under these conditions – namely that a government is by the very nature of things going to have to make decisions quickly about unexpected events that will *not* be unambiguously covered by previous instructions, and that many of these decisions will be irreversible – no amount of fiddling with the mechanisms of limitation will allow one to dispense totally with the phenomenon of a *certain* amount of discretion on the part of the holders of power. A variety of mechanisms of accountability and supervisions have been invented: antecedent or concurrent civic scrutiny to weed out undesirables (such as the Athenian δοκιμασία or the activities of someone like a Roman Censor), institutions of impeachment or recall, and collegial forms of the exercise of power in which each member has a veto over the actions of the others, retrospective investigation in which former magistrates are required to present an account of their actions and defend it at the end of their period in office (the Athenian εὔθυνα) with prosecution for deviance, and so forth. The strengths and weaknesses of these mechanisms have been the subject of intense discussion. Finally, however, at some point one will have to trust some officers to some extent; it is extremely hard to see how this can be avoided.[51] For liberalism there will always remain at best a tension between, on the one hand, the need to have a sufficient amount of discretionary power located in designated persons to discharge the necessary tasks for which government is instituted and, on the other, the desire to limit, define, and regulate that power.

It is extremely hard to know what position to take on Rousseau's claims that subjugation to personal power is more difficult to bear, and more morally reprehensible, than subjugation to non-personal forms of power, whether they be the power of forces of nature or the power of a fully rational set of universal laws. There is no doubt that an allergy against

---

[50] This is the 'can' of effective political possibility.

[51] The two theorists who have done the most to call attention to the phenomenon of trust and its role in politics are Annette Baier ('Trust and Anti-Trust' and 'Trust and its Vulnerabilities' both in her *Moral Prejudices*, Cambridge, Mass.: Harvard University Press, 1994) and John Dunn, 'Trust and Political Agency', in *Interpreting Political Responsibility* (Princeton: Princeton University Press, 1990) and 'Trust', in *The History of Political Thought and Other Essays*.

personal subordination is genuine and very widespread in the modern world. On the other hand, it is hard to know how much weight to give to this reaction, because we know that people can also have precisely the opposite experience. That is, they can find the very 'anonymity' of some modern forms of power, for instance of the global economic system, or of (as one says) 'faceless' bureaucracies, morally outrageous.[52] At least, it could be thought, one can sometimes appeal to an arbitrary despot and establish a minimally human relationship with him, even if one that is not satisfying. The tyrant at least recognises his victims enough to hate them; the multinational corporation acts *sine ira studioque*, using general principles of economic rationality. Some prefer the tyrant.

[52] A. Hirschmann, *The Passions and the Interests* (Princeton: Princeton University Press, 1977).

CHAPTER 3

Democracy and rights

I. DEMOCRACY: DESCRIPTION AND INTERPRETATION

This is not strictly a historical work, but still it might seem slightly odd that I have treated liberalism at such length without first discussing 'democracy'. The reason for this is that in the sense most relevant for contemporary political philosophy, liberal thinking is older than democratic thinking, although democracy as a political form is older than liberalism. Liberalism establishes itself as a coherent and self-conscious political and intellectual movement at the beginning of the nineteenth century, but 'democracy' as a self-conscious, theoretically articulated and defended, positively valued political ideal associated with a real political movement, is an invention of the very late nineteenth and early twentieth centuries.

To be sure, most political thinkers in the West have in some sense known about the early Greek experiments in democracy, and later also about the form of government practised in some of the Swiss cantons. However, there was no real continuity between any of these experiments and any concrete feature of the modern world.[1] Democratic systems were thought in any case to be completely unworkable in any except very small and undeveloped societies. In addition, it was always a peculiar feature of the ancient democracies that we have no extended theoretical discussion of them by a *supporter* which describes and analyses them in positive terms, trying to convince an audience that they are a good thing for theoretically respectable reasons. On the contrary, our knowledge of them comes from theorists who were overwhelmingly hostile (the Old Oligarch, Thucydides, Plato, Aristotle). So until the late nineteenth century 'democracy' is virtually a term of abuse.[2] Of course, once that

---

[1] S. E. Finer, *The History of Government* (Oxford: Oxford University Press, 1997), pp. 267–73.

[2] See J. Dunn, 'Conclusion' to *Democracy: The Unfinished Journey* (Oxford: Oxford University Press, 1992), pp. 239–66. See also C. Farrar, *The Origins of Democratic Thinking* (Cambridge: Cambridge University Press, 1988).

situation changes during the course of the early twentieth century the usual process of rewriting history anachronistically takes place. Historians begin trying to trace a purportedly single line from the Athenian Assembly, through perhaps certain Roman popular institutions (especially the *comitia tributa*), various medieval forms of communal self-government, the French Revolution, etc., and ending this march of glory in, say, the Constitution of the Fifth French Republic or the Federal Republic of Germany; this historical account, however, is grossly incorrect.

A further difficulty in treating 'democracy' results from a systematic ambiguity about what the term is supposed to designate. The 'state' is a set of really existing structures and institutions in the world (although these would not exist unless people had a certain set of rather highly theoretical views). 'Liberalism', on the other hand, is in the first instance a doctrine about politics, a set of beliefs with strong normative content. 'Democracy' shifts uncertainly.[3] Sometimes it appears to be a more or less normal descriptive term which designates one kind of institutional structure that can be picked out as distinct from others. Thus it may purport to designate either a set of institutions that does exist or did exist (or any set of institutions that are 'sufficiently like' the fifth-century Athenian Assembly or the early twentieth-century British House of Commons), or a set of possible social institutions which does not actually exist and did not exist, but which we now imagine or propose, and which is described in sufficient detail to allow us to imagine what empirical properties it would have (for example, proportional representation for central governmental functions and first-past-the-post elections for local councils). As such 'democracy' is a normal empirical term with an agreed-on usage which classifies existing regimes into recognisable types. This is true even if the term 'democracy' is used to designate something that does not, never did, and never will exist, just as 'Pegasus' purports to designate something which does not, did not, and probably never will exist.

However, in addition to this normal descriptive use of the term, 'democracy' and its derivatives are also used in a very different way to give a highly theoretical interpretation or explanation of what is going on in certain empirical political systems, or what ought to be going on, or why such systems are or ought to be highly valued. In this usage, 'democracy' designates a set of very highly normatively laden political ideals or desiderata. We are familiar with these ideals from the cruder forms of contemporary political rhetoric: democracy means that the people as a

---

[3] See J. Dewey, *The Public and its Problems* (New York: Holt, 1927), chapters III, and V.

whole – the whole population – has power or rules, the general will is supreme, the society is autonomous.

The contrast between the empirical and the ideal use of 'democracy' becomes clearer if one thinks of practices of criticism. We are familiar with claims to the effect that a certain political system or regime is not really 'democratic'. This form of criticism can be more or less radical, fastening on particular blemishes in the way the system operates or more general defects in its structure. At its most radical, it would be perfectly comprehensible – perhaps not *true*, but understandable – to claim that some feature which characterised most actually existing forms of democratic government and had never before been objected to, was not 'really' democratic, meaning by that that the feature in question was not really conducive to the rule of the people as a whole. Thus at a certain point in time one could claim that first-past-the-post forms of election were less democratic than systems of proportional representation, or one could revive the ancient Greek view that elections of any kind were undemocratic. The Greeks held this view because they optimistically assumed that in elections especially competent people would tend to be chosen; not everyone in the population, however, was competent. Finally, at a certain point one could claim that *all* forms of democratic government hitherto known were not 'really' democratic because they excluded women from suffrage. It is not a self-evidently true claim that the ideals of rule by the people will be best assured by any particular empirical system that one might care to specify, except perhaps the radical non-system of unanimous direct democracy. In societies which are at all concerned with 'democracy' there has been continued disagreement about how the relevant ideals are precisely to be specified, but also about how these ideals are to be implemented, that is about whether or not concrete political devices actually foster or embody the ideal. The interpretative path connecting an empirical specification of a set of institutions and even a set of relatively clearly and explicitly formulated ideals is itself virtually always going to be open to debate and disagreement.

Although it is analytically useful to try to distinguish empirical and normative components in the conception of democracy, one should not overlook the fact that in practice the two almost always coexist in an almost inextricable unity. Some theorists in fact have thought that this apparent conjunction of empirical and a normative component is not a defect we need to remedy or a vacillation which we ought to try to avoid, but rather a positive, potentially praiseworthy inherent characteristic of all the central terms we use in politics. Most of the more important human political institutions are not like natural phenomena, that have no inherent teleology, but rather are goal-directed. Political structures are things we produce and reproduce *because* we think they will have some desired properties, but usually these will include the aptitude of the institution in question to have certain effects or allow us to attain certain ends. Elections exist and continue to exist as institutions in our society because we participate in them and thereby reproduce them; we participate in them, neither because they are 'just there' nor because we simply like the experience of voting. We vote in elections because we think that this will be a good means to some end, such as giving power to the marginally less corrupt and ignorant of the available standing candidates for office, thereby slowing down certain reprehensible social trends, etc. I can continue indefinitely filling in further details of my own particular goals. This general because-structure is not an external imposition, but part of the nature of the thing in question. One does not understand the political institution in question unless one understands this about it, and it is this inherent teleological structure of central political institutions which makes certain common forms of criticism of them possible and potentially effective.[4] This argument against the view that institutions have *no* teleological properties is compatible with the Nietzschean possibility that they have more than one single effective aim, goal, or function. Even a superficial investigation will suffice to show that different people participate in elections for a number of different reasons.

Bearing in mind, then, that the empirical and normative dimension can be separated only analytically, let me begin with a brief discussion of 'democracy' in its more empirical aspect. The word 'democracy' means 'people's power', so presumably a political system is a democracy if in that political system the people holds or exercises the political power. Who, though, are 'the people'? Although it is neither completely clear what this means nor completely uncontroversial, let me assume that 'the people' means something like 'the mass of the (adult) population'. 'Democracy', then, means that the mass of the population has the political power in a certain regime. As an empirical concept 'democracy' can refer to any of at least three dimensions that are relevant to the way in which power is organised and exercised: (a) to the deliberative process, that is, the process by which various possible options for action

---

[4] This line of argument is strongest, perhaps, among philosophers influenced by Hegel. Thus Adorno thought it a major theoretical and moral deficiency of what he calls 'positivist' political science that it even tried to operationalise concepts like those of democracy. Cf. *Der Positivismusstreit in der deutschen Soziologie* (Neuwied and Berlin: Luchterhand, 1969), pp. 7–101.

are proposed, discussed, and their strengths and weaknesses evaluated, (b) to the actual decision mechanism by which a group chooses a course of action, and (c) to the execution or implementation of decisions. Further-more, in each of these dimensions, a distinction has traditionally been made between cases in which the people directly act along the relevant dimension and cases in which the people control, or could to a greater or lesser extent control, the actions of those who act. Usually systems with a high degree of direct action by the population as a whole along all three dimensions are called systems of 'direct democracy'. Systems of indirect control are usually called 'representative',[5] but I will also call them 'in-direct'. There are various mechanisms of indirect control. Some of these are proleptic and operate by using filtering devices of various kinds to determine which agents are to fill which positions of power. Elections are one such widely used device, purportedly giving the populace some indirect control over decisions by allowing it to choose who will make and implement those decisions. Others, such as various requirements of publicity, operate concurrently with the exercise of power. Finally, still others operate after the event: these include the prospect of prosecution for violation of given norms or expectations, or even, in some systems, simply for failure.

There can be different distributions of direct and indirect forms of the exercise of power. There are traces of some early systems in which there was direct action along dimension (b) above, but only indirect control of (a). Thus in the *Iliad* (II. 265ff.), only the nobles seem to be permitted to speak in the assembly. When the commoner Thersites tries to say something in debate, he is silenced and given a beating because he is not a noble. At the end of the debate, however, the actual decision is made by the mass of assembled troops who shout out their approval or disapproval.[6] The ideal-type of a direct democracy would be a political system with maximal direct elements in all three dimensions. Although in some societies close approximations of the direct exercise of these functions are realised, for any number of reasons direct exercise along all the dimensions is unlikely in a reasonably large and complex society. Not even fifth- or fourth-century Athens satisfies the strictest version of this, because in Athens there were functionally specified agents entrusted with the implementation of the decisions of the Assembly. There was a

---

[5] For an especially good recent discussion of representative institutions see B. Manin, *Principles of Representative Government* (Cambridge: Cambridge University Press, 1997).

[6] For a discussion of similar enlighteningly archaic practices in Sparta, see W. G. Forrest, *A History of Sparta* (New York: Norton, 1968), esp. pp. 40–68.

body of citizens responsible for executions and finally, one person who administered the poison to condemned citizens, and who (as we see from *Phaedo*[7]) had a certain amount of discretionary power – Socrates could apparently negotiate with him about when to take the poison. If there is delegation, rather than direct exercise of power, it is hard to see how a certain amount of discretionary power can be avoided If, however, one adds to the empirical specification of 'democracy' even some vague notion of the ideal which a democratic system is supposed to aspire to instantiate, then the discretionary power of a delegated individual, even in minor matters concerning the implementation of decisions, might be thought to be problematic.

Imagine in contrast to the *Phaedo* the case of a relatively isolated tribe. All the members of a village come together around the fire in the evening and talk 'freely'; they all agree that it will not do to have sexual relations with animals, that Ping has had such sexual relations with a sheep, and that he needs to be punished (even Ping takes their point and agrees: he is very sorry; he was lonely, the sheep was very cute). The punishment, they agree, is to be stoning. Each member of the tribe picks up a rock and throws it at Ping. Ping takes flight, being careful *not* to flee in the direction of the field where the tribe's sheep are grazing. Most people are careful not to hit him: he is a likeable chap, and, after all, a relative of virtually everyone in the village; some people can sympathise even more keenly with his predicament – they have seen the sheep and she *is* very cute – others do, of course, as their neighbours do, but feel no need to do it *con furore*. Two days later a chastened Ping discreetly slips back into a derelict hut at the edge of the village, and invites his favourite elderly classificatory 'aunt' to share a mess of chortleberries he has picked; this aunt, he knows, has always had a special fondness for chortleberries.[8] On the evening of the next day Ping is back at his usual place around the fire. There is no delegation in this case, and it does not make much sense to speak of 'discretionary power' – people just do what they want to do, and that is that. As the case is described, what people wanted was exactly what they got: Ping abashed, but not injured; the 'right' principles in one sense upheld, but without any serious disruption of harmonious social relations. If the power of executing decisions had been delegated to someone, it seems highly unlikely that exactly this effect could have been

---

[7] Plato, *Phaedo*, 116–17. See the excellent analysis by D. Allen, *The World of Prometheus: The Politics of Punishing in Democratic Athens* (Princeton: Princeton University Press, 2000), esp. chapter 9.

[8] The example is modelled on the description of 'punishment' for incest among the pygmies of the Iturbi forest in Colin Turnbull, *The Forest People* (New York: Simon and Schuster, 1972).

attained. The executioner would have had either to kill Ping or let him escape. If the executioner is not held in some way responsible to everyone in the camp for whatever happens, it hard to see how whatever decision is finally made by this delegated individual will be more than accidentally related to what the people of the village want. Even if the executioner is held responsible, this responsibility can be antecedently defined only in very general terms which will need to be interpreted to be applied to individual cases.[9] Again, it will be no more than an accident if the discretionary decision made within the space opened up by this looseness of fit between general directive and particular application exactly catches what the people in the tribe want.

As has been pointed out, the word 'democracy' means 'people's power' but it was earlier noted (chapter 1, § 2) that the concept of 'power' is ambiguous, meaning either the ability to do something in particular/anything at all, or the ability to get what one wants. Correspondingly, then 'democracy' should mean either a system in which the people have the ability to do some particular things/anything they decide or a system in which the people have the ability to get what they want. This ambiguity, which may have seemed to be no more than a scholastic bagatelle when it was first introduced, now exhibits perhaps unexpected political relevance. There does seem to be a rather significant distinction between a situation in which the mass of the population is able effectively to decide politically to embark on any course of action without any constraint or limitation, and the situation in which the mass of the population gets what it wants. This is particularly the case if 'what X wants' is interpreted as meaning 'what X *really* wants'. It is sometimes not in principle difficult to determine what a given human individual wants in a particular well-defined context – if I am tired, I want to have a sleep; if you take my bicycle, I want it back – but it does become less than perfectly straightforward to say *in general* what even an individual wants. The reasons for this are too obvious to require expatiation. To specify not just what I generally want, but what I 'really' want (with an emphatic 'really') is a dauntingly formidable, perhaps even impossible or incoherent, task.

Hard as it is to say what an individual wants, transferring or extending this to a group, in particular an ill-defined group like 'the people', compounds the difficulty. To speak of 'the people' wanting anything is already to construct for them a will, and construe them as a single

[9] As above, p. 107.

subject.[10] To speak of them as having real interests or real wants is to make a very strong and highly theoretical claim. The idea of a fully self-transparent, unitary self that could have any notable properties is dubious in its application to individuals, and even more so to groups. If I speak of the people as 'wanting' something, and at the same time reject this model of some kind of unitary self, then what exactly do I mean? To say 'they must want X' because a majority of their representatives voted for X – even assuming that this is true – is not informative in the right way because the appeal to 'wants' was supposed to be some kind of enlightening interpretation of what was happening when the electoral mechanism was operating *correctly*, not just a restatement of what actually happened. Or rather, the appeal to real wants was supposed to give us a place to stand at a distance from the actual operation of politics from which we could possibly evaluate whether or not some particular mechanism of decision and implementation was giving the right outcome – actually giving people what they wanted. We cannot do that if 'what they want' is just defined as what the mechanism operates to produce. If that is what 'they want X' means, I can just delete references to wants altogether and describe the outcome of whatever processes resulted in the decision in question. One should not, of course, underestimate how important and how difficult it is actually to specify how it is that a certain political decision comes to be made and implemented. To take a particularly crass and notorious example: how exactly did the Nazis decide on the Final Solution? Who did what, when, and to what effect? Even more mundane cases that were less consciously shrouded in secrecy are not without problems: how exactly did the poll-tax become 'what the British people want' in a certain year? Describing the mechanism and specifying the historical path by which this came about are both difficult and important, but they do not automatically tell us anything about 'the people's' wants.

In any case, one might think that the idea of a community in which people are clear and in agreement about what they want is not an ideal of a political system: politics is about getting things done when people do not agree. This does not imply that one can never sensibly speak of 'real interests' or of what 'the people' want (or really want), provided one specifies the particular empirical context relative to which one makes the claim.[11]

In well-defined cases like those of ancient cities it may not be at all confusing to speak of an oligarchic or democratic political system, because

[10] Schumpeter remains indispensable on this topic: *Capitalism, Socialism, and Democracy*.
[11] This is the topic of chapters 2 and 3 of my *The Idea of a Critical Theory*.

'oligarchy' and power there had a concrete reference. The oligarchy was not an intangible, abstract, virtually invisible 'power-elite' (à la C. Wright Mills)[12] which required considerable theoretical sophistication even to discover, but a group of two or three dozen men who walked around the streets in clean clothing, married only each others' daughters, discussed affairs with one another and sometimes ordered their servants to beat particular other people up. Although the members of this group might sometimes disagree with each other about what policy the city should adopt, there were times at which there was nothing unclear about who these people were, what they wanted, or what power they had. Similarly 'democracy' had a concrete reference. It did not connote a vague gesture to the theoretical authority and the large but unspecified powers of an abstract entity: 'the people', but designated a highly particular group of smelly unkempt Hellenic subjects who lounged around, eating chickpeas and ogling boys on the side of a particular sunny hill in Attica, when they weren't out engaging in what was often not much more than a form of large-scale piracy and extortion in various places around the Mediterranean. In the twenty-first century we can afford the luxury of looking back on all this with indulgence or even affection and admiration because they often used the loot to build nice temples, but at the time it must often have been no fun at all to be in their immediate vicinity.

Among the various ideals associated with democracy one can, then, distinguish two: (a) the people have the power in the political system, in that whatever gets done is something *they* do directly, and nothing gets done except what they do – they make the decisions that are made (and execute them), and (b) the people can get what they really want or what is really in their interest.[13] One reason to be interested in (a) would be because one thought it was conducive to (b), and I might think that (b) was desirable because I might think that it was in general a good thing for people to be able to get what is in their interest. This line of argument depends on the claim that being able to do what you want is conducive to getting what you 'really' want, and it is at least highly questionable that that is always the case.[14] It is also, of course, an open question whether it is always *good* for a person or group of people to get what they 'really' want. However there could also be completely different reasons for supporting (a), independent of any assumption about the relation between

---

[12] C. Wright Mills, *The Power-Elite* (New York: Oxford University Press, 1956).

[13] What people really want and what is in their interest may differ on some analyses. The issue of the relation between these two is of great importance for politics.

[14] Plato, *Gorgias*. See above, pp. 23–4.

(a) and (b). For example, one might think that giving people power to decide political questions did not in the least in itself conduce to helping them get what they really wanted or what was in their real interest in any particular individual case, but that the experience of having and exercising power, and seeing that one had this power in the long run, focused people's minds and made them get clearer about what they really wanted. Or one might think that visibly giving people power prevented them from blaming anyone else when some particular decision had notably unpleasant consequences; in this way it might be thought to be conducive to social peace and stability. In any case it is clear that emphasising (b) as the important element of democracy, and simultaneously taking a very robust line on the distinction between what people really want and what they decide to do, may bring one to some harsh conclusions, such that in some circumstances – for instance, where the populace is immature – the most democratic procedure will be to put decisions into the hands of an individual who knows what is truly in people's interest, and brings it about. This, in turn, might motivate liberals simply to reject the whole distinction between what people really want and what they merely seem to want. Giving up on this distinction leaves the arguments for direct democracy intact, but it deprives indirect democracy of some lines of support that have been thought important for it.

In summary, then, one might think of democracy as meaning either (a) that the 'people' (however defined) actually does what gets done (direct democracy) or (b) that the people has (some indirect) control over what gets done (through mechanisms that are to be specified), or (c) that the people gets what it really wants.

2. DEMOCRACY: EVALUATION

I have spoken of the ambiguity in the meaning of the term 'democracy' as between a description of a set of existing institutions and an ideal. Now I wish to take a step back from that discussion and distinguish three different approaches to democracy with the intention of evaluating it. In the process I will investigate reasons which we might have either for preferring it to other forms of political organisation or for having reservations about it.

The first of these is an external and instrumental approach, which is not inherently a moralising one, although it may not be strictly non-evaluative. This is, as it were, a 'political science' approach. It asks: what are the properties of this kind of political regime? How does it arise and maintain itself? What dangers threaten it? What are its advantages and disadvantages? This approach, which exists in several variants, concentrates on an existing designated set of concrete institutions, mechanisms, and political structures (such as majority-rule voting, a multi-party system with first-past-the-post elections, etc.) and investigates the various properties which such systems will be likely to have, including properties that might be relevant to evaluating these practices and institutions. In fact, of course, we will pick out the aspects of the political system we wish to investigate relative to our own conceptions of what is valuable. Given, therefore, that we value human survival, peace, efficiency, continuity, we will tend to focus our attention on features of particular mechanisms that seem to be most relevant to this, but we may also have various moral or imaginative requirements that we wish to see realised in our political system – we may want it to conform to our conception of justice, to embody certain aesthetic properties, or to express who we are.

Thus, on the positive side, many have emphasised the utilitarian advantages of 'democracy' (i.e. the standard Western European system of multi-parties and regular elections to representative parliaments) as a way of maximising the likelihood of smooth transitions in the transfer of power from one group to another. If the warrant to exercise power is flexible in democracies, depending on the contingencies of voting, even a group that is going out of power may not be motivated to use force to retain it, thinking that their day will come again. Others have emphasised the general social advantages of making decisions after the widespread social discussion that is characteristic of many forms of democracy. There have been thought to be two ways in which such discussion is advantageous. First, it would increase the chance that as much relevant information as possible was brought to bear on the decision. Second, some theorists, such as J. S. Mill, have thought that such extensive public discussion would have the effect of making people more tolerant, and that this is an advantage.[15]

On the negative side, five criticisms have been levelled against democracy. First, it has often been claimed that democracies have great difficulty in pursuing long-term consistency in policy making. Direct democracies may change their policies with every meeting of their defining Assembly, and even indirect democracies with every election. This property will be especially inexpedient when a democratic society is engaged in long-term competition with societies that are less whimsically directed.

[15] Mill, 'On Liberty', pp. 52–4.

Second, liberals like Constant have pointed out that the operation of a direct democracy is extremely onerous and time-consuming, more so than would be easily tolerated by a modern population, who are more interested in their private affairs than in politics.[16] On the other hand, representative democracy can under some circumstances increase this existing inclination on the part of the populace to withdraw from politics. This is a loss for the individuals in the population because they are deprived of a fundamental component of the good life, the chance of developing their powers in an important sphere of public action; it is also a loss for the society as a whole because it leads to a politics of irresponsibility.[17] Third, it is a long-standing objection that democracies devalue human knowledge. They may, to be sure, in a superficial sense maximise the information available, but, by putting the opinion of the fool and the expert on an equal level, they effectively nullify the possibility of bringing relevant expertise optimally to bear on outstanding issues.

Fourthly, in many circumstances J. S. Mill's view that public discussion in democracies leads to toleration may seem dementedly optimistic. Thus de Tocqueville points out that free public discussion can have the effect of polarising and radicalising opinion, rendering positions more inflexible, and reducing the space available for tolerance and compromise.[18] Experience strongly suggests that the more one learns about the reasons which others have for their views, the more one sees that they are a tissue of culpably self-serving illusions, self-deceptions, and deeply rooted prejudices – just as one's own are, if seen with sufficient dispassion, or from the outside. In addition a fuller understanding of others' views often leads one to see them as immovably trapped by history and circumstance. Although this may increase both one's understanding of why people feel the need to hold the views they hold and the personal sympathy which one might have for their plight, it also tends to make it clear how restricted the possibilities of peaceful consensus-based change are. It might become clear that in very many cases only violent, large-scale upheaval, or reeducation in that 'long-run' in which, as Keynes noted, we are all dead, could actually change established habits, attitudes, preferences, and beliefs. Whether or not understanding and discussion in the short term (say, twenty or thirty years) are likely to increase

---

[16] Constant, 'De la liberté des anciens comparée à celle des modernes', pp. 502–6, 509–12.

[17] Constant, 'De la liberté des anciens comparée à celle des modernes', pp. 512–13.

[18] A. de Tocqueville, 'De la démocratie en Amérique', in *Oeuvres, papiers, et correspondances*, ed. Méyer (Paris: Gallimard, 1951).

'tolerance' is a question that depends on the existing balance of power in society, one's assessment of the possibilities for radical change through the application of violence, one's independently held private moral beliefs and temperament, and a variety of other empirical factors.

Max Weber is responsible for developing the fifth line of criticism.[19] Democracy, he thinks, is incompatible with one of the basic requirements of modern social life. Weber believes that in a large modern society with a capitalist economy all organisations will have a tendency to become bureaucratic. This will be as true of political organisations as of private corporations. The basic principles on which a bureaucracy functions, however, and its prevailing ethos, are directly contrary to those that prevail in a democratic political system. A bureaucracy is essentially an administrative system that operates according to fixed, antecedently known rules; it is hierarchical with well-defined areas of competence for each functionary. Bureaucrats have access to information and power only conditional upon satisfying strict criteria. Democracy, on the other hand, as a political ideal, and direct democracy as a form of political practice, is inherently anti-hierarchical and egalitarian. Furthermore, in its purer forms, democracy is, if not explicitly anti-nomian, at any rate anti-regular. That is, democracies do not exist in order to follow existing rules, or even necessarily to give themselves new sets of *rules*, but rather to make *new* decisions. The basic principle of a bureaucracy is: Those with the necessary qualifications and authorisation will meet and follow the rules. The basic principle of a direct democracy is: the whole people will meet and they will do what they want. There is a certain late twentieth-century tendency to see democracy through the anachronistic haze of fashionable Kantianism, and this obscures the distinction between the logic of democracy and the logic of bureaucracy. Weber was relatively immune to this and was very keenly aware of the fact that Kant himself was both an opponent of democracy and an anti-liberal. It is only a slight exaggeration to say that Kant is in fact, if anything, rather the philosopher of bureaucracy than of democracy. Unless one accepts some of the more dubious aspects of Kant's metaphysics there is no reason to think that the people in ruling themselves must, will, or ought necessarily to do so through universal rules.[20] It is a mistake to think that Weber is 'against' bureaucracy, or that he thinks that it is no more than a a necessary evil. Rather bureaucracy has outstanding virtues.

---

[19] See Weber, *Wirtschaft und Gesellschaft*, pp. 854ff, also 'Politik als Beruf', in *Gesammelte politische Schriften*.

[20] See R. Bittner, *Moralisches Gebot oder Autonomie* (Freiburg and Munich: Alber, 1983).

Some of these virtues are of a kind to make it, rather than democracy, especially attractive to liberals. Thus, the rule of law is a bureaucratic, not a specifically democratic ideal, and liberals who are concerned with the defence of privacy can only applaud the bureaucratic principle that certain information about individuals which must be collected in order to allow a modern state to function is to be accessible only to those with special qualifications and authorisation.

The second approach to democracy focuses not on such relatively instrumental advantages (and disadvantages), but on the purportedly inherent moral superiority of democratic procedures. This line descends from Rousseau, and has become part of the common coin of narcis-sistically adulatory self-description on the part of 'democracies'. The highest moral demand, according to this view, is that a person be free and self-legislating, and avoid dependence on the will of others. The only way to avoid such dependence in a complex society is by a process in which people institute a self-legislating political system. Democracy deserves moral approbation, because in a democracy the people have the (political) power, and to say that the people have the (political) power is to say that they form a self-legislating community of the requisite sort.

Often this view is associated with a strong distinction between what is merely instrumentally good (that is, good for something else) and what is good in itself (or good for its own sake). For people to have the power to decide for themselves what they will do is a good in itself, so even if democracy were to turn out to be inherently inefficient, ill-informed, corrupt, bad at allowing them to satisfy basic welfare needs, it would still have an absolute moral advantage over other forms of politics. Adopting the distinction which I made above in chapter 3, § 1, pp. 118–19, one could say that since self-legislation is a good in itself, it is in people's real interest; at the deepest level what they really want, or perhaps what they really ought to want, is to have and exercise the power to decide themselves, even if it does not allow them to satisfy their other interests. The two senses of 'power' would, then, collapse into one.

In its full Rousseauist form this approach depends on a set of metaphors about the human will, individual wills and a purported 'gen-eral will' which is directed at the common good. It requires a considerable amount of imagination and strong discipline in suspending one's disbelief to accept Rousseau's account of the 'general will' as a correct description of anything that actually exists in any society known to us.[21] One can

---

[21] The negative part of Schumpeter's account has not been bettered since it was originally published; see Schumpeter, *Capitalism, Socialism, Democracy*, pp. 250–68.

live a full life as citizen of a country with democratic institutions and never vote at all, or vote assiduously and never succeed in voting for any candidate who ever wins public office, meanwhile actively disapproving of most of the major policy decisions of the successive governments in power. If I am in this situation I may have various good reasons to applaud the fact that I live in the state in which I live and I may even welcome the fact that that state has a moderately democratic political system, but if I am reasonably reflective these good reasons will have nothing to do with some fantasy that this system is really *my* will writ large. Another way of putting what is, I think, the same point is that 'self-legislation' refers either to each human person ('positive freedom of the individual' in the terminology I used above in chapter 2, § 3), or to the society as a whole ('positive freedom of the group'). For this approach to succeed, one would have to argue for the categorical moral standing of the positive freedom or self-legislation of the group, a similar standing for individual self-legislation, and some coherent connection between the two. The relation between individual and group self-legislation, however, is anything but clear.

This third approach to democracy is one which in the modern period was pioneered by Dewey.[22] This approach emphasises the *epistemological* significance of democracy as a form of organisation of collective action.[23] What is important about democracy, on this view, is neither its strictly instrumental contribution to the realisation of various exogenous goods such as social stability, peacefulness, and welfare, *nor* a purported inherent moral superiority derived from the fact that it is a realisation of human autonomy. Rather, democracy for Dewey is a good form of political organisation because it is the appropriate political modelling of a more general form of human interaction which has both epistemological and valuative advantages, and which finds its best realisation in a free scientific community devoted to experimental research. Just as such a research community is trying to invent theories that will allow us to deal with our environment in a satisfactory way, so a good human society would

[22] See Dewey, *The Public and its Problems.* There are recent treatments by R. Westbrook, *John Dewey and American Democracy* (Ithaca: Cornell University Press, 1991) and Alan Ryan, *John Dewey and the High Tide of American Liberalism* (London: Norton, 1991).

[23] Dewey was an opponent of 'epistemology' as a purported free-standing philosophic discipline, but he was also convinced of the need to understand as clearly as possible how systematic forms of human knowledge arose, developed, and were applied. See his *The Quest for Certainty* (New York: Minton, Balch & Co., 1929), esp. chapters 5 and 7, and 'The Experimental Theory of Knowledge', in *The Influence of Darwin on Philosophy* (New York: Holt, 1910). If one strips 'epistemology' of its traditional philosophical sense, one need not disapprove of adjectival usages of derivatives of this term to characterise Dewey's position.

be one that was a kind of experimental community devoted to trying to discover worthwhile and satisfying ways of living.

Science, Dewey thinks, has been cumulative over the past few centuries in that it has constructed theories that give us greater and more exact control over the world. This has been widely acknowledged. What has not been so widely recognised, though, Dewey believes, is that the most important way in which science has been genuinely and cumulatively progressive is not through the accumulation of more and more useful, new, individual theories, but through the development of new and better methods for discovering and testing hypotheses. Viewed from sufficient historical distance, Dewey thinks, science must be seen as a historical process in which two things happen in conjunction: theories are invented, tested, and used, and new methods for the discovery and standards for the evaluation of theories are invented, tried out, and refined. We accept theories because they have been developed using the most appropriate available methods, because they satisfy our relevant standards of evaluation, and because they work (i.e. allow us to do what we wish to do with the theories in question); we use the methods we do because they have shown themselves to be efficient in allowing us to come up with acceptable theories. To put it in a way that is perhaps misleading, for Dewey there is no such thing as '*the*' scientific method. The methods used by science, are not a fixed and unchanging given, but rather a shifting set of techniques that themselves have a significant history and develop progressively and unexpectedly in the course of enquiry.[24]

Dewey now proposes to think of a human society as a group involved in a similar two-sided activity of trying, on the one hand, to discover how to attain or realise the life that is desirable and, on the other, to determine what is, or could be, meant by 'desirable'. The two sides are intimately connected (if the process is taking place in a healthy and unconstrained way). This process can best flourish in a society with 'democratic' institutions; that is Dewey's claim. The advantages of democracy are not merely instrumental (as in the first evaluative approach) nor is democracy strictly 'good in itself' regardless of consequences (as in the second evaluative approach). Rather Dewey rejects the distinction between the instrumentally useful (what is good 'for' something else) and the inherently valuable (what is good 'for its own sake') as a fundamental building-block of thought.[25] Some theorists, developing views that can be found

---

[24] J. Dewey, *Logic: The Theory of Inquiry* (New York: Holt, Reinhardt, and Winston, 1938), pp. 1–41.
[25] Dewey, *The Quest for Certainty*, chapter 10. See also J. Dewey and L. Trotsky, *Their Morals and Ours* (New York: Pathfinder Press, 1973).

in the ancients and Rousseau, thought that democracy was good in itself; others that a democratic society was good for its effects. Dewey thinks both groups are in a sense right. The democratic structures of a free society, he thinks, are both experienced as good (= satisfying) in themselves and are conducive to further goods.[26] Furthermore, social processes in such a society will render the distinctions between instrumental and inherent value, actions performed for their own sake and those performed for the sake of something else, and prudential means-ends-thinking and moral thinking increasingly irrelevant.

This last point about the distinction between the merely instrumentally good and that which is inherently or categorically or absolutely good in itself marks a watershed in political thought which has not, I think, received the attention it deserves. Kant, Max Weber, and Habermas think that this distinction is sharp, and designates a basic and ineluctable feature of human thought and experience. Hegel, Marx, Dewey, and Adorno, on the other hand, think that the distinction is relative and contextual, and that it is a sure sign of a deficiency in a society if this distinction is given too much prominence or taken too seriously. For Marx and Dewey, the distinction is a remnant of a primitive state of society in which slaves did the instrumentally necessary work, and parasitic aristocrats pursued the good for its own sake. The distinction between means and ends, things good in themselves and good for something else, intrinsically good and good for its consequences, or inherent and instrumental value is a distinction one can perfectly well make *within* and relative to a certain established context of thought or action, but it is neither a fundamental nor an absolute distinction. What is a means in one context, may be an end in another, and in many spheres, especially those in which human activity is freest, the distinction will have only whimsical application. The members of a non-demoralised orchestra may make their living by playing so that to some extent they play for the sake of the money they earn, but the music they make may also have inherent value for them. In a fully developed and free human society most human action would be performed both because of the good effects or consequences it would have and because it was experienced as good 'in itself' by the agent.

The great opponent of this Deweyan view is Kantianism, because Dewey claims that the virtue of democracy lies precisely in its being, like science, radically open, with *everything* – assumptions, results, methods, standards of evaluation – in principle subject to revision. It is especially

[26] Dewey, *The Public and its Problems*, chapter v.

important for Dewey that even the methods which are used to try to discover what scientific theories are most useful and what the good life is, are themselves things that are, or should be, seen to be amenable to change. There is to be nothing fixed as being beyond discussion, no absolute a priori, nothing set down in stone prior to investigation, nothing which can count as a certain, pre-existing categorical obligation; everything is contextual, provisory, and subject to revision in the course of enquiry.[27] Although Dewey presents his view as a theory of democracy, he tends not to distinguish very clearly between democracy and liberalism. In any case this aspect of it – his view about the essentially fluid and open nature of a good society – is perhaps better understood as formulating one of the points at which a basic impulse of liberalism and democratic values coincides. The deepest incompatibility between liberalism and democracy, on the one hand, and Kantianism, on the other, is not the often-remarked sado-masochist tenor of his ethics,[28] but his view that knowledge and morality require fixed a priori frameworks.

Dewey's 'democracy' is about as abstract and as far from the concrete original sense of the term[29] as it is possible to get. It is not very clear what kind of state is envisaged by this account. It may not be an accident that Dewey usually speaks of a democratic 'society' or of 'community', and not of a democratic state.[30] Perhaps Dewey's 'democracy' is not at all intended as a concept with application to the political system of a state, but as the idea of a liberal community which, like ancient direct democracies, lacks state-structures. If such a liberal community is supposed to be like a flourishing scientific community of experimentation, it would not be surprising to discover that it lacked a full-blown state-structure (i.e. an agency which monopolises legitimate coercive violence and whose members are not fully voluntary subjects), because we normally think of a scientific community as a free and voluntary association – that is supposed to be its nature, and surely it is Dewey's intention to conform to this intuition. A state by its nature is not free. So either (a) Dewey's liberal community will not have a state (and so it certainly will not be an indirect or representative democracy), or (b) our conception of an

---

[27] The best discussion of this is Dewey, *Logic*, esp. chapters I–IX. Cf. also Stuart Hampshire *Justice is Conflict* (London: Duckworth, 1999).

[28] See H. Heine, 'Zur Geschichte der Philosophie und Religion in Deutschland', in *Beiträge zur deutschen Ideologie*, ed. Meyer (Frankfurt/M: Ullstein, 1971); Adorno and Horkheimer, *Dialektik der Aufklärung*, Excursus II; J. Lacan, 'Kant avec Sade' in *Ecrits* (Paris: Seuil, 1966), vol. II; A. Baier in 'Moralism and Cruelty: Reflections on Hume and Kant', in *Moral Prejudices* (Cambridge, Mass.: Harvard University Press, 1994).

[29] See above, pp. 117–18.

[30] Dewey, *The Public and its Problems*, chapter V.

experimental (scientific) community will shift so that we can conceive of such a community as having a sub-sector which is coercive, and/or there will be a shift in our conception of what counts as 'coercion' (or both (a) and (b)).

Now that we have discussed liberalism and democracy, it might be useful to take a look back at the state, to see how it fits into the liberal, and into the democratic project. We spoke of the state as an abstract structure of authority located in a socially separate and distinct institutional sphere which had certain coercive powers at its disposal. In the modern period its powers seemed to increase so dramatically that it became an object of fear; on the other hand, it was not easy to see what alternative there was to the state form of organisation. To fear what seems overwhelmingly powerful and inescapable is not perhaps the best of starting points for disciplined reflection. One can distinguish five ways of reacting to the state.

The first is the radical democratic reaction. The idea here is that one can prevent the state from coming to confront its subjects as a fearsome, alien force, and that one can do this by putting state-power in the hands of the populace as a whole. In this respect, radical democratic theory is a continuation of the Jacobin line of argument discussed earlier. One form of this approach is theoretically unobjectionable: that is the return to an extreme form of direct democracy of the type found in fifth-century Athens, or rather to a form of democracy that is an even more extreme version of that because comprising full participation of all the adults who live in a certain geographic area (not excluding women, slaves, and long-term resident aliens). This would prevent a state-structure from getting out of the control of the populace, but it would do that by virtue essentially of abolishing the state as a separate institutional structure. For the reasons originally given by Constant – modern states are too large to be direct democracies, and in any case modern people want to pursue their private lives and be spared the need to run the political system directly – most modern theories assume representative parliamentary institutions as the basic mechanisms of democracies. Elections, caucuses, procedures for impeachment or recall, or for the implementation of the occasional plebiscite, can no doubt offer some temporary and limited reassurance, but do not deal with the underlying fact that any individual or finite group of individuals in a modern state with representative democratic institutions is still confronted with a massive apparatus of coercion that is not directly biddable.

The second reaction is embodied in what I will call the *étatiste* view, which is that for a variety of reasons (with different theorists giving different ones priority) it is essential or highly advisable to have such a distinct locus of power and authority. Thus one might think that in a world populated by *other* states, many of them predatory, it is essential for the minimal self-defence of a certain population that it be organised as a state, or one might think that it was necessary to have an independent power that could intervene in the economy to prevent it from self-destruction, or we might think it desirable to thwart the popular will in some cases and prevent it from expressing itself in the form of direct action, such as lynchings, pogroms, riots. Part of the whole point of having such a free-standing coercive structure (the state) is that it be independent; local popularly controlled police forces, after all, usually join in the pogrom or at least stand aside and remain 'neutral'. As long as this basic fact remains, there is *always* going to be a gap between the political power of the state and the effective powers of the populace, and, on this argument, that is a good thing.

While some of the institutions of representative democracy may be valuable in a variety of ways, and some of the more extreme forms of democratic rhetoric (self-rule, positive freedom, the General Will, etc.) may serve as a useful social-psychological emollient, reconciling people to their *de facto* subjugation to a structure which has much more power than they do and does not always have their individual best interests at heart, the hope that the state-power could ever really be 'our' power or fully under collective control is completely misplaced. One of the points of having police is that they can face down the local lynch mob. The police serve *this* function perfectly well even if they are the agents of a highly authoritarian and non-democratic central government. That means, though, that if the state as an institutional coercive apparatus which is beyond the control of its members has a rationale at all and is going to continue to exist, then the moralising ideal of full Rousseauean political autonomy is illusory, and it makes sense to be pragmatic about political arrangements. Whether more or less 'democratic' political institutions are appropriate is a question that is best answered by reference to a variety of different considerations, and in some cases less 'democracy' might be a perfectly reasonable political goal.

The third reaction is that of anarchism. Anarchists believe that the state is neither necessary, efficient, useful, nor morally justified. They

assume that it would be good simply to abolish the state-structure altogether along with all its powers of coercion. This refreshingly non-evasive
and clear-eyed *theoretical* position is marred only by the inability of people as they are now constituted to aspire to the complete abolition of
the state and envisage an acceptable alternative form of social organisation. To be sure, it might be true that if the state were to be abolished
under relatively propitious conditions, people would then either come
to realise that they could flourish in anarchy even without changing
their basic dispositions, values, habits, beliefs, or they would find their
'nature' so radically transformed that they judged their final state more
satisfactory than life in a state. This, however, is not a possibility that is
likely to have much, if any, rhetorical or persuasive force under present
circumstances.

The fourth reaction is a Marxist one. Marxists differ from anarchists
in that they distinguish sharply between the functions and powers of the
state and the institutional embodiment of these functions. The central,
major functions of the state – forms of co-ordination of human action
on a large scale, if necessary by coercive means – are, Marx thinks, genuine exercises of developed human powers, and the development and
exercise of human powers is a good. For Marx these powers can be exercised in a variety of different ways and by different socially organised
institutions at different times in history. The state, as a particular kind
of institutional structure, is only one, historically specific way in which
these functions can be exercised. To the extent to which the state is actually effective in exercising these functions and in developing associated
powers, it is historically 'justified'. Marxists, of course, also believe two
further propositions. First, they hold that the state now no longer discharges its appropriate function well. Many of its more striking coercive
activities in the form in which they came to be exercised by the late nineteenth century are gratuitously repressive; they are not only no longer
necessary for progressive economic development, but they actually hin-
der such development.[31] Second, Marxists believe that there could be a
reorganisation of economic life which would allow us to continue to exercise and develop the organisational capacities which have historically
had their locus in the state, but to do so without preserving the state as
a continuing distinct set of social institutions. The powers of the state
can be, in the words of the early Marx, 'reappropriated' by the society
as a whole.[32] The powers remain intact and are even developed; the

---

[31] See G. A. Cohen, *Karl Marx's Theory of History: A Defence* (Oxford: Oxford University Press, 1978).
[32] Marx, *Marx-Engels Werke*, Ergänzungsband 1, pp. 539–40; also vol. I, 'Zur Judenfrage'.

structure which originally brought them forth can wither away as a distinct sector of human society. The most plausible model for this would seem to be that of a series of councils composed of all the immediate producers in local units of production. These councils would organise production, legislation, and the administration of public order in a unitary way; there would be no distinct 'police', 'courts', 'parliament', etc. Anarchists thought that this was merely a new name for the same old state oppression, or an even worse form of repression, and that as long as the accumulated coercive powers remained, it did not really much matter where they were 'located'.[33] If Marxists believe in the withering away of the state apparatus with relocation of the state powers to society as a whole (economically appropriately organised), anarchists will be satisfied only with an atrophy of the coercive powers themselves.

The fifth reaction is that of liberalism. Liberalism begins from a general deep suspicion of the democratic programme: the tyranny of the majority in a democracy can be as great as that of any monarch, and in one sense it is more subtly dangerous than despotism because it can give itself a more plausible moral veneer. If the state cannot by appropriate institutional means be transformed into a simple and harmless extension of my own freedom and self-governance, it is potentially oppressive, and the more it can present itself (falsely) as such a form of my own freedom, the stronger its hand in the rhetorical debate, and the more potentially noxious it is. The institutions of representative democracy give apparent ideological warrant to state activities, but no real control over them. In such circumstances the appropriate political attitude is to try to protect individuals by building defences against potential encroachments by the state. Such bulwarks can be institutional or theoretical, or both. One way in which some forms of liberalism have tried to discharge this theoretical task of defence of individuals is by appeal to a theory of 'rights'. Partly this is a work of propaganda, of talking up the theory of rights; partly an attempt to institutionalise individual 'rights' in the political and juridical system. For one of the most widely influential forms of liberalism, individual 'rights' are to constitute the bulwark against which the waves of state intervention will break in vain.

4. LEGAL RIGHTS

That liberalism stands in at best a highly strained relation to the state, and to 'democracy' (or, at any rate, to any of the more consistently

33 See R. Tucker (ed.), *The Marx–Engels Reader* (London: Norton, 1978), pp. 542–8.

developed forms of democracy), has often been noted. It is, however, an important fact that the connection between liberalism and a theory of 'rights' is also historically adventitious.[34] There have been political theories based on a notion of inherent individual human rights that have been anything but liberal in their conception and execution; Hobbes argues from a theory of such rights to a form of political absolutism. There have also been historically influential and theoretically highly reflective forms of liberalism that have eschewed recourse to rights altogether, or even thought that the idea of a human right was nonsense (e.g. the liberalism of some utilitarians or of Dewey).[35]

Although a recognisably modern use of a concept of 'rights' antedated by several centuries the development of anything that could reasonably be called 'liberalism', still rights-discourse itself is not a very old feature of Western political thought and the idea that such a rights-discourse could be the free-standing and universal framework for much of politics is a very recent idea indeed. Our modern notion of a (subjective) right as a particular collection of individual entitlements is essentially feudal in origin. More exactly, it is a feudal transformation of a concept that derived from Roman private law, that is, in particular the law of property transactions between individual citizens. In feudal society private ownership of territory or land or a manor can carry with it certain public functions such as police powers, powers of administration and jurisdiction, etc. This originally feudal notion that ownership is connected with jurisdiction then eventually comes to be connected with a more specifically modern idea that all individuals are equal and should be seen as being autonomous and having prima facie moral and political jurisdiction over themselves. This is given a biological/legal gloss when I am said to be my own master by virtue of automatically or naturally owning (i.e. having property rights in) my own body. I have, then, (private) property rights in my own body; that ownership is construed as giving me jurisdictional powers over myself, such as the power to decide what can be done to my body (= me). In this way self-ownership can be thought to be the origin of moral claims, etc. The story of the growth of rights-discourse and the story of liberalism are two conceptually and historically distinct stories that touch each other tangentially at various points, until in the immediate aftermath of

---

[34] The history of the concept of 'rights' in infinitely complex. For the early modern period see Richard Tuck, *Natural Rights Theories: Their Origin and Development* (Cambridge: Cambridge University Press, 1979). J. Waldron (ed.), *Theories of Rights* (Oxford: Oxford University Press, 1984) gives a good overview of some recent philosophical discussion of rights.

[35] See J. Waldron (ed.), *Nonsense upon Stilts: Bentham, Burke, and Marx on the Rights of Man* (London: Methuen, 1987).

the Second World War a particular conjunction of the two establishes itself as the ideology of NATO and the United Nations and from that position begins gradually to infiltrate the rest of the world.

A proper understanding of the concept of 'right' as it is now used requires one to make two distinctions. The first of these is the distinction between 'objective' and 'subjective' conceptions of 'right'. The easiest way to begin to grasp this distinction is to look closely at the two distinct grammatical structures in which claims about 'right' are often couched.[36] On the one hand, we can say 'it is right that . . .' where the blank space following 'that' is filled in by a clause, for example, 'it is right that the severity of the punishment be commensurate with the gravity of the crime', 'it is right that the laws of God take priority over those of men', 'it is right that innocent bystanders not be needlessly endangered by police operations', 'it is right that relatives share the prey of a successful hunter equally'. I take grammatical expressions of the form 'It is right to . . .' where a verb follows, as variants of the same kind of usage. Thus 'it is right to increase medical provision in this area', 'it is right to equalise the tax burden', 'it is right to make peace now', etc. A third, similar expression is: 'It is right for . . .' e.g. 'it is right for colleagues to get along'. This conception is called 'objective' because the judgement about what is right is made, as it were, from the point of view of a spectator and judge who looks at features of the (social) world from a distance and from outside the particular perspectives of the human agents engaged in any given transaction. This viewpoint is not one which begins by fixing responsibilities, powers, or sanctions on any one of the participants, and in fact someone who adopts this point of view may never proceed to assign such responsibilities for action to particular agents.

The features of the world which are relevant for specifying what is 'right' in this sense will not, perhaps, be 'objective', if one uses that term in the way in which some metaphysicians have used it. These features will not refer only to what used to be called 'primary qualities' and they will usually be constituted by human actions. It will, however, in general be possible to characterise what would be right in a situation from an internal perspective on individual human agency. From the fact that it is right to treat equal cases equally, nothing *inherently* follows about how this state of affairs that is right is to be brought about, if it does not exist, who is responsible for acting in what way to bring about what is right, and so on. Knowing that we are at war and that it is right to make peace,

---

[36] The grammatical distinction is not an infallible marker of the distinction between objective and subjective conceptions. I use it here merely as a first approximation.

does not necessarily give me a clear idea of who, concretely, is to do what to whom in order to realise what is right. The situation can be described in a way that does not inherently connect it with subjective moral and motivational features of any of the particular agents involved in it. 'It is right that . . .' does not make explicit reference to any particular human agency. Even saying 'it is right for colleagues to get along' does not in itself assign responsibility for failure, duties to remedy, or in fact any other concrete requirement for individual human action.

In contrast to this, we often speak of particular people having or possessing or owning rights. Here, the basic grammatical form is a substantival, not an adverbial, usage of 'right': 'I have a right to . . .', not 'it is right that . . .'. This is called a 'subjective' conception because it starts from some particular individual subject, attributes to that subject a power and/or warrant, and then moves out from there to the relation of that subject to other subjects and other features of the world. This conception of a 'right' is one in which the 'right' in question is thought to be inherently related to the particular subject who is considered to have or own it. An 'objective' right refers to a state of the world (which is good or bad, laudable or wrong); a 'subjective' right to and entitlement, that is, to an action (or omission) that I (or some other designated subject) can/should/ought to have the power or warrant to perform or suffer. Built into the notion of a subjective right is that of a designated agency that is the centre, locus, and bearer of it. If *I* have a right to a certain piece of property, then one at least knows something about how action to remedy any violation of that right should be directed. If my bicycle is stolen, action should be directed at restoring the bicycle to *me*. If you stole it, you should return it to me.

To some extent one can find parallel subjective and objective versions of certain claims. Thus, there would not prima facie seem to be much difference between 'I have a right to sell the produce of my garden on the open market' and 'it is right that Raymond sells [or: is allowed to sell?] the produce of his garden on the open market'. We may in general suspect that the range of states of affairs it is objectively 'right' to hold is wider than the class of subjective rights. Thus many people have argued that it is 'right' that animals be treated decently, although they have also thought that only human subjects, or at least subjects who are capable of language and thus of *asserting* and claiming rights, can be thought to have rights. Animals as non-humans could not, then, be construed as bearers of subjective rights. On the other hand, one might think that every assignment of a subjective right must have as its analogue an overarching conception to the effect that it is objectively right that this person or corporation have that right. Even this can be questioned. Perhaps Shylock has a right to his pound of flesh, but it may not be right that he exercises this right.[37] Despite this, it is clear that the basic way of looking at the political process which will be most naturally embedded in one of these conceptions is very different from that most naturally associated with the other.

When people speak of the 'recent' origin of rights discourse they have in mind specifically the discourse of *subjective* rights, or the idea that individuals have or own powers or warrants to do or refrain from doing or suffering, and that these have some reliable epistemic, moral, and political standing. The attribution of 'objective right' is as close as it is possible to come to a cultural universal, if one understands the idea of 'right' sufficiently widely to include any kind of normative assessment of what features the world ought to exhibit, and one construes 'objective' in a non-metaphysical way. Every human society has *some* views about how the social world ought to be organised, how people should act, and so on. In this sense of 'normativity' the normative is a feature of every society known to us. It is right to brush one's teeth after eating. The Greeks in the Homeric period thought it was right to cremate the dead; later Greeks thought it was right to bury them. It is right to initiate the exchange of greetings with acquaintances encountered on the street (unless one can see that they are engaged in an immoral, illegal, or embarrassing activity). This of course doesn't imply that 'normativity' is to be understood in the specifically Christian or Kantian form. It is a natural confusion brought on by linguistic accident and the prevalence of the subjective conception of rights in our time and society to think that this omnipresence of phrases like 'it is right that ...' or 'it is right to ...' implies that the concept of a subjective right is equally deeply rooted in the human condition. That is not the case. The idea that individuals can 'have' rights is a specific historical invention of the late middle ages in the West, and the experience of Western antiquity (and virtually the whole non-Western world until very recently) shows that it is in principle perfectly possible to conduct social life at a high level of civilisation without the idea of a subjective right. China has done without this idea very nicely for the past several thousand years.

The second distinction or set of distinctions which it is useful to make when thinking about rights is that between what are sometimes called 'positive' or 'legal' rights and other kinds of rights, especially those rights

---

37 One would be tempted here to distinguish legal from moral rights. Shylock has a legal right to the pound of flesh, but it is not morally right for him to exercise this legal right. See also below, p. 139.

which are called 'moral rights','natural rights', or 'human rights'. This
distinction cuts across the previous distinction between subjective and
objective conceptions of right. One can have a subjective or an objective conception of legal right, and one can also have a subjective or an
objective conception of human rights. The notion of a 'natural right' is
now usually used to mean a 'natural subjective right', and the notion of
such a natural (subjective) right is very different from the notion of what
used to be called 'natural law'. Natural law is a purported normatively
binding principle governing (perhaps among other things) humans and
their relations with each other, and which has its origin in certain facts of
nature, the will of God, or the dictates of reason.[38] It in no way follows
from the assumption that there is a natural law that the form this natural
law takes will be one which attributes subjective rights to individuals;
such a natural law would be just as likely to be couched exclusively in
terms of what is objectively right.

It is easiest to begin with the concept of a legal right.[39] To speak of
a legal right presupposes the existence of some kind of legal system.
'Law' itself is a term used very widely to refer to a variety of different
form of human action, procedures, codes, institutions, etc. To simplify,
I will assume that the legal system in question is of the kind familiar to
us from civil and criminal proceedings in Western European countries
during the past hundred years or so. Here the decisions of legislators are
connected with relatively efficient and visible systems of enforcement
and execution. If the legislature has decided that it is right that adults
with more than two children should pay a special higher tax-rate, then
there is a system of courts, tax officials, and (eventually) policemen who
can be expected to enforce this decision. This gives a clear sense to the
claim that in *this* place it is (objectively) legally right that adults with more
than two children be taxed at a higher rate: the appropriate authority
has made that decision, it is properly recorded (probably in writing),
and the appropriate administrative and police forces are implementing
it. Similarly, if I am said to have a (subjective) right to ownership of this
house, this means that I have a deed which will be recognised in the right
court *and* that there is a mechanism, the police, that will act to prevent
certain things from happening – passers-by from turning me out of doors,

---

[38] On the politics of 'natural law' see John Dunn, 'The Dilemma of Humanitarian Intervention', in
his *The History of Political Theory and Other Essays* (Cambridge: Cambridge University Press, 1996).

[39] Actually of one especially central kind of legal right known more technically as a 'claim right'.
The discussion of types of legal rights that has become canonical is W. Hohfeld, *Fundamental
Legal Conceptions as Applied to Judicial Reasoning* (New Haven: Yale University Press, 1923). He
distinguishes four types of rights.

neighbours from stabling their animals in my sitting-room against my will, etc. – or at any rate give me some form of redress. The mechanism for redress need not function in an absolutely infallible way, and we know of past legal systems in which the mechanism for enforcement was in one sense very informal indeed. Thus it is said that in Iceland the law-speaker spoke the law and people could go to law with one another and get what amounted to a clear and definitive answer to some disputed legal question at issue – yes, it was *not* right for Sven to burn down Knut's farmstead and Sven should pay compensation. Nevertheless, there was no effective mechanism for enforcing the legal decisions, apart from public pressure and (as a last resort) outlawry. Oddly enough, though, in the long run social solidarity (and certain facts of geography) was sufficient to make outlawry work as an effective punishment. To say that the system of redress is through a series of sanctions (public disapproval, avoidance, outlawry) which are themselves weak, diffuse, and informal is not to say that a mechanism for enforcement is non-existent, or that one can make sense of 'law' and 'right' in abstraction from the idea of sanctions.

Obviously the 'sanctions' invoked and applied might be formal, but their real burden might not be visible and externally coercive. In certain societies religious groups might administer a religious code through formal procedures, including a series of courts which imposed spiritual sanctions, such as exclusion from participation in certain rites. The exclusion is a visible and may be a coercive result, but the real force of the measure, for believers, is to be deprived of various intangible spiritual benefits. In principle one could imagine a formal procedure that imposed *merely* intangible sanctions. The religious court which saw itself as the final and definitive arbiter of salvation might simply declare someone a 'vessel of iniquity' or a 'child of abomination', irrevocably condemned to perpetual spiritual blindness and perdition. It might then be thought unnecessary to proceed any further. Why bother excluding the condemned from social participation in the church, religious ritual, etc.? In fact the presence of the spiritually stigmatised might be thought to have a salutary effect on those who are still potentially saved. Although there was no visible and tangible force to this sanction, it might work as a sanction if all those involved firmly held the appropriate religious beliefs. It would not work as a sanction on people who did not believe. Magic is said by some anthropologists to be like this: it works very well in a society in which virtually everyone believes in it, but will not work either for or on those who do not. Cases like this, then, are not counterinstances to the claim that for us to speak of a legal system there must be some clear and specific notion of sanctions. Failing such a system of sanctions, there is nothing but a set of diffuse individual and collective moral feelings.

Positive laws define certain rights one way or the other relative to the granting of certain forms of redress or remedies, but many people also believe that positive legal systems are not in themselves normatively self-validating, and they are certainly not self-enforcing. Since no legal system is self-validating, it makes sense at least in principle to ask the question whether the 'rights' recognised and enforced by a given positive legal system are or are not the ones it 'ought' to enforce. In the first instance our own individual moral intuitions and theories give us a standpoint from which to evaluate any given legal code or system. We can judge that although the legal system says that this state of affairs x, y, z is 'right', actually a very different state of affairs 'α, β, γ' is right (and ought to be recognised as such by the legal system). It is clear what 'right' means in its first occurrence in the immediately previous sentence. It means that a certain state of affairs will be the object of attempted implementation by the existing mechanism of redress and remedy. It is, however, not so clear in what sense the term 'right' is being used in its *second* occurrence (except to designate someone's moral judgement), because *ex hypothesi* 'right' in its second occurrence is *not* being used to refer to something that will be taken care of by any of the existing mechanisms.

5. HUMAN RIGHTS

There are two slightly different ways in which the existing system of positive laws can fail to be aligned with my own moral or normative conceptions. First of all, my moral views may extend not only to various easily discernible, repeated kinds of actions that people perform, but also to relatively ambiguous forms of human behaviour, to various psychological attitudes that people might have, and so on. My moral views might also include parts in which I gave especial consideration or weight to actions that were done 'freely'. By 'freely' here I would mean that they were done despite the fact that they were in no obvious way socially sanctioned. Thus I might think it morally a good thing for a person to exhibit gratitude in some contexts, but I might also think (a) that 'gratitude' was not the kind of thing that could be regularised, that the form it takes could vary, and that it could be difficult to tell whether a given course of action was an instance of it or not, and (b) that gratitude had value only if freely given (or had greater value if freely given). For reasons like this, I might welcome the fact that the legal system as a system of external application of potentially coercive mechanisms was not applied to certain areas of human life, and thus did not fully map my moral views.

Some philosophers have, then, been tempted to distinguish two kinds of 'rights': first the legal rights set out in a positive code with clear mechanisms for enforcement, and second a ghostly analogue of this in the form of a set of 'moral rights'. My benefactor has no legal right to my gratitude, but – some might want to say – he or she has a 'moral right' to it. To produce a fuller parallelism with the clear case of legal rights, one might even invent a mechanism of 'moral sanctions', in that Lady X will destroy my good opinion of her or at least put it under strain, if she fails to be grateful to a benefactor. The loss of my good opinion (or my adverse moral judgement on her) is thought to count as an informal sanction, not fundamentally different from the kinds of social-avoidance behaviour, and denial of reciprocity, which figure so importantly in the organisation of simple, and some not so simple, societies.

The second way in which a set of legal rights can fail to be fully aligned with my moral beliefs is that it can sanction something which I think ought not to be sanctioned, or it can fail to protect adequately some human interest which I think ought to be legally protected. Or, finally, it can fail to sanction legally something I think ought to be sanctioned legally (and not, for instance, just morally). A legal system which attempts to ensure religious uniformity by burning heretics will not correspond to the moral and normative views of post-Voltaireans, and a society which enforces compulsory redistribution of land every few years may violate the normative conceptions of those who believe in absolute individual property rights. This may lead people to hold that there is a system of 'natural' or 'human' rights which is *prior* to the given positive legal code and (in the cases in question) with which that given legal code is incompatible. People have, it might be claimed, a natural human right to freedom of religious belief and property, a right that is logically prior to or at least independent of any existing legal code, and it is by appeal to this set of natural human rights that one can effectively condemn some legal systems.

One can make a terminological distinction of a sort between the use of the term 'natural right' and the use of the term 'human right'. 'Natural right' seems to be used in philosophical contexts, when what is at issue is the grounds on which the purported rights hold – they hold 'by nature'. Most modern versions of this understand it to mean that it is a right that can be discovered by reason operating on some very basic facts about nature, 'human nature', and society. A 'human' right, in the first instance, is simply a right all humans possess. The phrase 'human right' is generally used in the context of international politics, and refers in the first instance not to the source or grounds of validity of the purported right in question ('nature') but to the domain of its application ('to *all human beings*'). Nowadays it is invoked when we wish to intervene in the internal affairs of another country of whose regime or policies we disapprove.

Assuming for the sake of argument that one wished to speak of 'natural' or 'human' rights at all, there would seem to be no inherent reason why the set of natural rights might not extend beyond the class of all humans. One might want to attribute natural rights to animals, if one thought humans had such rights. One reason for restricting legal rights to humans was to maintain a connection between having a right and being able to *claim* that right by speaking in a certain way in a court. The notion of a 'natural right' is not self-evidently thus bound to the conditions of empirical litigation, so it is not clear that this reason would be sufficient to deny that animals had natural rights. On the other hand, why could one not hold that (some) natural rights were restricted to a subset of all humans? Thus in many traditional views parents might have natural rights of control over their children and husbands over their wives, but these were not natural rights that were common to *all* humans. On the other hand, one can easily imagine a *legal* system which assigns to all human beings rights without making any claims that these rights are 'natural'. In addition, even if one admits that there can be 'rights' that are not tied down to a specific legal system, one need not think that such rights had their ground in nature or reason in any very obvious sense of these terms. Still, despite this, I will follow what seems to me the prevailing usage and assume that when one speaks of 'human rights' one has in mind a natural right all humans have, simply by virtue of being human. In particular, I will assume that a 'human' right is an individual subjective right each human has simply by virtue of being human.

The doctrine of natural rights has been subject to a number of criticisms. First, some have thought that there is something objectionable about it because many of the traditional 'natural rights' are negative, and there is something ontologically derivative or valuationally undesirable about taking something negative to be fundamental. This does not seem to be a very plausible objection. Many traditional natural rights, it is true, are rights to exclude people or prevent them from doing things. This might seem to be true of such things as property rights which are in any case central to many conceptions. To say I have a property right might be thought to mean that I may exclude others from making use of my item in the world without my permission. Similarly many civil rights might be construed as barriers that prevent the state from interfering in my life in various ways. Even if this construal of many such rights were correct, though, there would still be no reason in principle, assuming that one did accept the existence of natural rights, not to include in the list of such rights positive rights, such as a right to a minimal level of welfare, a right to engage in certain basic human activities, and so forth. In addition, one might wonder whether the distinction between positive and negative even applies sharply to many kinds of recognised rights. Finally, even if the ultimate list of rights one recognised was merely negative in some discernible sense of 'negative', it is not clear what exactly would be wrong with that. At the very least the onus of specifying defect is on the person who brings this kind of objection.

A second criticism is that rights are entitlements. This can be thought to be grounds for objecting to a rights-based approach, because a political philosophy based on the assignment of entitlements to people could be thought to encourage them to become too passive. One might appeal to the Humboldtian argument about '*Selbsttätigkeit*'[40] as a goal to support this line of argument. A variant of this criticism might claim that an excessive focus on rights as entitlements made people too greedy, too self-centred, or too irresponsible. Sometimes defenders of this critical tack suggest that recognition of natural rights must be accompanied with a corresponding recognition of natural duties. Again, the basic difficulty with this line of thought is that although natural rights are perhaps conceived, by those who think they exist, as entitlements, there is no particular reason to believe that they must be construed as entitlements to receive benefits passively. They may perfectly well include such things as a natural right to participate equally in politics, or to come to the aid of those in need across existing political boundaries.

A third criticism is that the doctrine of natural rights is inappropriately individualistic. The bearers of natural rights are human individuals, not groups, and one might have two objections to a political philosophy that was oriented around such a structure. First of all, one could be an opponent of individualism for any one of a number of general moral or philosophical reasons. Second, one could think that groups were in some sense ontologically or phylogenetically prior to individuals and that it was appropriate for this fact to be reflected in the basic structure

---

[40] See above, pp. 81–2.

of one's political theory. Even today all human beings are still born as members of groups, and this has been the case for as far back as we care to trace human history. The hominid pack is older than the capitalist entrepreneur or the modernist artist. Oddly enough, Marx, who was one of the most consistent critics of rights discourse, did not criticise it because of a purported individualistic bias; he seems rather to have thought that the problem with rights is not that they were too individualistic, but that they contributed to maintaining an economic and political system that allowed too little room for the development of human individuality.[41] Furthermore, as with the first two criticisms, although historically significant collections of purported natural rights have generally been collections of individual rights, there is in principle no reason why one could not assign natural rights to groups, or even to non-human features of the world. Thus, for instance, animals might have a right not to be killed, a painting a right not to be destroyed, or a glacier a right not to be melted. Since the notion of a natural right is from the start no more than a moralising conception about what would be desirable without any concrete specification of an enforcing agency, there seems no particular reason to exclude woods, mountains, or other inanimate objects from the realm of purported natural rights.

To be sure, attributing natural rights to groups would tend, I think, to undermine part of what has traditionally made the doctrine of 'natural rights' psychologically attractive to people. The general strategic point of a doctrine of purportedly natural rights was to give one a point of view rooted in 'nature' which was prior to and independent of the vagaries of particular social, legal, and political systems, and which would allow one to criticise particular existing legal and political systems.[42] If, however, one allows from the beginning the assumption that groups might have rights, one must immediately ask questions about the internal structure of groups. Who has the right to speak for that group, and appeal for the implementation of the right? Does the chief speak for the tribal group? Do only democratic or anarchic tribal groups have a right to survive as distinct societies? This would mean that specific and highly contentious political questions would enter at the level of analysis at which natural rights were originally recognised, rather than later. If the whole point of the doctrine of natural rights, however, was to reach a

---

[41] See Marx, 'Zur Judenfrage', in *Marx-Engels Werke*, vol. I; also 'Die Deutsche Ideologie', in *Marx–Engels Werke*, vol. III, esp. pp. 74ff, 423f.

[42] See J. Dunn, 'Rights and Political Conflict', in *Interpreting Political Responsibility* (Princeton: Princeton University Press, 1990), esp. pp. 53f.

level of analysis that was prior to that at which such real-world political questions could even arise, proceeding in this way would tend to destroy the psychological attractiveness of the approach. If one starts raising and answering normative questions about the proper forms of social and political organisation here at the very beginning of the analysis, why not just go straight on to a theory of the form of politics required by natural morality, bypassing the issues of rights altogether? So it seems that one can save the doctrine of natural rights in this way, but only at the cost of undermining its rationale and appeal.

A fourth criticism is one that is directed at the nature of a 'natural right'. In what sense can these purported natural or human rights be called 'rights'? Is it, as I have strongly suggested, essential to the existence of a set of 'rights' that there be some specifiable and more or less effective mechanism for enforcing them? Earlier historic periods in the West were in a more comfortable position with respect to 'natural human rights' than we are. In some earlier periods it was possible to believe that there were natural rights, despite the fact that such rights were manifestly not in any way enforced in the real world. Furthermore it was possible to believe this without giving up the idea that possible enforcement through sanctions was essential to the notion of a right. Theological beliefs made all of this possible. God, it was believed, would enforce these rights,[43] even if no one else on earth did. One might get away with violations of the rights associated with fair dealing or gratitude to benefactors here on earth, but eventually God would see to it that one paid. Even earlier, when conceptions of nature were very different from those we have now, it might even have been thought that nature itself would enforce these rights. It is not completely crazy to imagine that there could be some rules for human action that were, as it were, enforced by nature itself.[44] Thus the rule not to drink too much alcohol in some sense enforces itself naturally. This does not mean, of course, that no one ever violates the rule, but then it is also not the case that the rule which many societies have against secret, premeditated murder of other members of the tribe is never violated. We can, nevertheless point to a naturalistic 'enforcing agency' in the form of the hangover which is nature's way of telling us – too late – that we have violated a rule and at the same time the punishment for violating it. It might be the case, as Plato seems to have thought, that by acting badly toward those around one, one condemns oneself to

---

[43] John Dunn, 'The Dilemma of Humanitarian Intervention', in *The History of Political Thought and Other Essays.*
[44] See J.-J. Rousseau, *Emile ou de l'education* (Paris: Garnier, 1964), Book II.

living in the society of people who have become bad people.[45] Living among such people is one's punishment. It is, however, hard to believe that anything like this kind of 'natural' connection can be expected to serve as an effective mechanism of enforcement for anything beyond the most rudimentary system of rules for human living.

Either there is or there is not a mechanism for enforcing human rights. If there is not, it would seem that calling them 'rights' simply means that we think it would (morally) be a good idea if they were enforced, although, of course, they are not. A 'human right' is an inherently vacuous conception, and to speak of 'human rights' is a kind of puffery or white magic. Perhaps if we repeat claims about natural rights long enough and loudly enough, and pass enough resolutions, people will stop doing various horrible things to each other. Indeed, perhaps they may, but perhaps not. The point about magic is that the particular nature of the formulae used and the names of the spirits invoked ('rights', 'the will of God', nature) matter less than that those on the receiving end *believe* in the reliable efficacy of whatever is invoked. To say that all humans have a natural or human right to self-determination, although the Indonesian government effectively prevents various groups in the archipelago from determining for themselves how they wish to live, means that we think the Indonesians *ought* to allow some groups to determine their own political life and we *wish* there were a mechanism which could be invoked to ensure this outcome. But, of course, there is not, and the powers-that-be in Indonesia know that there is not – that is the assumption of the whole train of thought.

'Group X has a natural right to Y' in contemporary political discourse, then, usually means that they do not have a (legal) right to Y but we think they ought to. To be sure, such things as the Universal Declaration of Human Rights are intended to establish a mechanism which *would* in fact bring it about that there were reliable consequences of suppressing free speech, preventing self-determination, incarcerating without cause, and so forth. However, it is important to realise that *even if* (and it is a cyclopean 'if') it *were* to be or come to be the case that such Declarations had more than rhetorical effect, they would constitute not so much a vindication of the doctrine of human rights as a transformation of individual components of someone's moral beliefs into a system of *positive* rights. We would merely have begun to invent and impose on the nations of the world a new layer of positive (international) law.

[45] *Apology*, 24c–26b.

I am not for a moment suggesting that we cannot invent a new legal system attributing to individuals and groups 'rights' which we announce our intention to implement, nor am I arguing at the moment about whether it would be a good thing for such a positive system of international law with an effective mechanism for implementation to be established. Whether or not it would be a good idea would depend on who was running the system and how. To institute such a system would require the means for speedy regular armed intervention in the 'internal' affairs of all the political groups that now exist on earth. Although it seems politically highly unlikely that such a state of affairs will, or even could, be brought about in the foreseeable future, it is not strictly impossible. The question is not whether this is possible or whether it would be a good thing, but whether such a development is the invention of a new set of positive 'rights' in a new international legal system or the emergence into visibility of a set of natural human rights that already existed. If we do implement certain 'rights' then, of course, they will exist just in the way in which all other positive legal rights exist, but they will exist because we have made them exist. The point, however, of appeal to 'natural or human rights' was to be that they were not supposed to be something we made to exist, but something we discovered which served as the grounds for judging actual legal rights, and thus relative to which we could criticise some existing system of positive rights. The only thing that can serve that purpose seems to be the flickering light of our variable moral beliefs. If we have enough strength we can make others care about our moral beliefs, but if the doctrine of 'natural rights' means no more than that we are powerful enough to make people careful not to do things of which we disapprove, then it seems no more than a theoretically obfuscating name for a well-known and not necessarily particularly edifying fact of power politics.

Again it is easy and comprehensible that those who have religious beliefs in a moral, omnipotent deity who is concerned with and rules the world can think there might be natural rights prior to any given legal code. Such a deity can enforce that system of 'rights' through various sanctions. Thus it is comprehensible and coherent to claim that 'all humans are endowed by their Creator with certain inalienable rights' (US Declaration of Independence, 1776), but the coherence depends on the assumption that the Creator exists and takes care to enforce the rights. Without the assumption of a (Christian style) creator the claim one finds, for instance, at the beginning of the influential book by Nozick,

Anarchy, State, and Utopia,[46] that people have rights and there are certain things you cannot do to them without violating their rights, is *just* the announcement that one proposes to build a castle in the air.

The term 'right' has two clear, but distinct senses. These are, first, the 'objective' sense (that is 'right' which we think ought to be the case or ought to be done), and, second, the subjective sense (I have a right if I have a claim backed up by an effective mechanism of implementation). It does not contribute to clarity of understanding to run these two senses together in the way that is characteristic of the discourse of human rights. If the cash value of 'X has a human right to Y' really is: 'we think that it would be a good idea for there to be a reliable system of effective power to enforce X's claim to Y (even if there is not such a system)', then it is only a moral belief. It would be well, however, to recall two of the basic features of the realm of politics. First, our moral views are not universally shared; people disagree about the good and the right. Second, even if people do agree or can be made to agree, such moral agreement *in itself* will not guarantee effective action.[47] This is not, of course, to say either that individuals have never in the past and will never in the future agree on *any* moral issue or that people never act on their moral beliefs or that widely shared moral beliefs might not sometimes have very significant political consequences. From the fact, though, that one rejects what has come to be called 'realism' in political theory – the view that moral beliefs never matter – it does not follow that even shared beliefs *reliably* translate themselves into predictably appropriate action, and that is what is at issue here. This fourth objection is lethal to the whole idea of a natural or human right.

6. RIGHTS AND POLITICS[48]

There are no natural rights. This does not imply that we cannot institute a system of (subjective) legal rights, and enforce it universally for all human beings, although to do this would require having a recognised legal and police system with effective jurisdiction and control over the whole population of the world. This is unlikely to occur unless all humans attain a level of moral uniformity that is now manifestly absent. Furthermore, although such uniformity is a necessary, it would not be a sufficient condition for constructing such a system of effectively enforceable

[46] *Anarchy, State, and Utopia* (New York: Basic Books, 1974), p. ix.
[47] Olson, *The Logic of Collective Action.*
[48] I am particularly indebted to Hilary Gaskin for discussion of the topics treated in this section.

rights.[49] Finally, even if such a system were to have been put in place, that would not make the rights we enforced 'natural' in any interesting sense of the word. They would then be 'positive'. None of this, perhaps, strictly implies that it is a mistake to think about politics in terms of natural rights or of 'rights' *tout court*; perhaps 'rights' are a convenient self-reinforcing fiction. I will suggest rather that they are an inconvenient fiction.

Thinking about the social and political world in terms of rights encourages illusory assumptions of stability and predictability. This is exactly what makes it useful in the short term and in well-defined political contexts of the peaceful operation of social institutions, especially in commercial and criminal legal cases, in the realm of the courts and the police. It is also what makes doctrines of 'rights' psychologically attractive. It is, however, also exactly what makes 'rights' an especially poor model to employ in reflecting in general about society and politics, at least if one aspires to attain any more comprehensive and illuminating understanding of the human world.

One major psychological motivation for introducing and holding fast to the concept of a subjective 'right' is a fear of the counterintuitive consequences of certain types of consequentialism, particularly utilitarianism. There is nothing, at least initially, in utilitarianism to prevent us from trying to attain the greatest happiness of the greatest number by radical redistribution of existing goods. In fact, not only is there nothing to prevent this, it is rather part of the original programme of utilitarianism: entrenched, merely traditional rights – for instance individual property rights – ought not to be allowed to interfere with the maximisation of the social good. Examples that are brought to bear against this view include cases like the one in which by killing me and redistributing my bodily organs, one could save the lives of ten persons who would otherwise die. To cater for the greatest good of the greatest number in such a case seems clearly to require that one person – me – be killed, or as we would be tempted to say 'sacrificed', in order to save the other ten persons. Rights theorists attempt to block this inference by claiming that each individual has some inviolable rights, for instance, a right to bodily integrity, and that these rights are 'trumps' in that they may not be overridden in the name of greater social utility.

This approach might seem to have some plausibility if one were living in a world in which purported legal 'rights' were not in fact very often 'officially' overridden or suspended. No country in the world fails

49 Olson, *The Logic of Collective Action*.

to punish in one way or another those who commit certain crimes, particularly crimes of violence. Punishment often includes actions that violate some of the most commonly posited rights, particularly the right to life (through capital punishment), or the right to freedom of movement (through incarceration). To reply that these rights are really not absolute rights *to* . . . life, freedom of movement, etc., but rather rights to continue to live and move about freely, *except* if one has been convicted of certain crimes through 'due process of law', seems, first of all, to make the rights seem more like privileges that are allowed to citizens who have merited them by their good behaviour. Second, it seems to require that one be able to specify rather more clearly than anyone has yet done what exactly 'due process' means, and what it is about certain crimes that carries with it loss or suspension of rights. Third, this way of proceeding might seem to many to come very close to being a way in which the rights of individual criminals are overridden in the name of greater social utility. One way of getting rid of the threat to public order posed by murderers is to execute them or lock them up.

Finally, it is not only at the conclusion of various criminal proceedings, but also in a wide variety of other situations, that rights are routinely suspended. Virtually all states will have provision for overriding individual rights in times of natural disaster, civil unrest, or armed foreign invasion. One will not be permitted to prevent the emergency services from crossing one's land to reinforce a dam which is about to break or to control an armed gang that is conducting an insurrection. Most states will have emergency legislation, provisions for proclamation of martial law or of a state of siege, rights of eminent domain, etc. These seem to be cases in which social utility is thought to outweigh legal rights. We may prefer not to think about cases like this, and in affluent, highly organised societies we can perhaps often afford this luxury, but it is hard to believe that we shall escape paying a high theoretical price for averting our gaze in this way.

In addition, if one moves from legal rights to the purported 'natural rights (of individuals)', how is one to construe the fact that these purported rights may massively clash with those of others? It is all very well and good to say that I have a natural right to secure enjoyment of my property, meaning that the society will intervene to restrain anyone who encroaches upon my peaceful enjoyment, but what can be meant by saying that each individual has a natural right to life, when there is one place left in the lifeboat and five remaining passengers on the ship who are unprovided for, or one final litre of water and two hundred people dying of thirst? Who exactly has the trumping 'right' there? What exactly is the point of ascribing 'rights' in situations like this? Perhaps saying that each has a natural right to life one means no more than what Hobbes seems to have meant, namely that no one can have good grounds for criticising me for trying to do what I can to continue to live. If two people both have such a natural right to the last place on the lifeboat, then one cannot criticise either one for taking that place and consigning the other to death by water. Still, it is not at all clear that appeal to purported 'rights' will tell you anything either about what will in fact happen in this situation or even about what ought to happen. Ascribing 'rights' seems completely otiose and pointless. Furthermore, it seems likely that the more rights one recognises, the more likely they are to conflict, especially in a world with limited resources. This inflation is already well advanced at least in industrially advanced countries.

Rights discourse might, thus, be a tempting *general* way to think about society if one had a fantastically optimistic view about God, the world, natural resources, and the avoidability of conflict. Imagine a world in which a divine Creator produced sufficient resources to support the life, liberty, freedom of movement, etc., of all its inhabitants, and wanted each human creature to make full use of these resources. In addition, the Creator would see to it that certain principles for the use of these resources were observed by punishing – perhaps in some way that was inscrutable to us in detail – violation of these principles. Perhaps Locke saw the world in this way at the end of the seventeenth century.[50] Unfortunately, this imaginary world is not at all like the real world we inhabit, if only because our real world does not seem to have sufficient resources to ensure for each human being a life in which even some minimal set of purported 'natural' rights is realised. Conflict about those 'things' to which people are supposed to have 'natural rights' – life, liberty, meaningful work, etc. – is real, endemic, and absolutely irresolvable by appeal to rights themselves. The real political organisation of the planet into competing states, each one itself divided into haves and have-nots, certainly multiplies these conflicts and renders them even more intractable than they would otherwise be, but does not create them out of nothing. If irresolvable conflict between bearers of purported 'equal rights' is throughgoing and unavoidable, what is the point of recourse to rights?

We can have good reasons for setting up our society to include a mechanism of barriers and powers granted to individuals to protect what we allow to be in their vital interests. Proposing a particular set of rights

[50] See J. Dunn, 'What is Living and What is Dead in the Political Theory of John Locke?', in *Interpreting Political Responsibility* (Princeton: Princeton University Press, 1990).

is always a strategic decision. Whether or not any particular proposal is appropriate is a question for political judgement. There are no algorithms for political judgement.[51] As far as we can judge on the basis of the available historical and sociological knowledge, any such system will always in fact be something provisory, and the barriers themselves will not be absolute. It is not news that I can lose my right to life or freedom in many countries by murdering someone, and in times of political crisis or serious civil conflict it is common for even very deeply rooted rights to be suspended: *habeas corpus*, due process, freedom of movement, confidentiality of transmission of information, not to mention the usual property rights. Few armies in the world permit full exercise of existing civil rights. One can expect freedom of speech, or association, or the freedom to engage in political activities to be suspended or overridden on submarines, missile bases, and nuclear weapons plants.

If there were convincing and clear philosophical grounds for speaking of 'rights' that were independent of the contingent, shifting conjunction of political expediency, institutional convenience, and our moral views and feelings, all of this might not matter. It would simply mean that the 'rights' in question were more complicated than we thought, and perhaps came into conflict with other rights more frequently than we thought. Since, however, that is not the case, and rights discourse lacks a coherent rationale, this *de facto* variability, frailty, and flimsiness of the system is important. The stability which a system of rights provides can in any case easily be exaggerated, and to the extent to which such a system is relatively stable and robust, one might suspect that the reason is the general well-groundedness or inertia of the wider political and social system within which the rights are embedded. The fact that a system of rights is an insubstantial and clearly derivative construct, dependent for its continued existence on a wider political and social framework, ideally one of economic prosperity, domestic and international peace, and stability, is an excellent reason for trying *not* to couch one's final political philosophy in terms of a doctrine of rights.

The idea of a natural, human right is neither well formed nor well grounded. Nevertheless, we can expect with reasonable confidence that rights discourse will continue to flourish. Fully to understand why this is the case, why rights discourse has such a hold on contemporary thinking, would require a large-scale investigation, probably with a strong empirical component, but two possible reasons immediately spring to mind. First, an economically advanced society will be understandably obsessed

---

[51] I am indebted to Zeev Emmerich for discussions which helped me to clarify my views on this topic.

with efficiency, predictability, and security, especially in assigning powers and responsibilities for the control of economic assets. This in itself is, naturally, by no means a criticism of it. The economic system provides us with the basic means of life and for this reason alone, if for no other, as long as we have no confident alternative to it, it behoves us to ensure that it works as efficiently as possible. Assigning individual ownership rights to economic factors is obviously a highly useful way to attain the goals of predictability, transparency, and efficiency. In a situation in which this form of legal-economic rationality is seen to be of the greatest importance and held in high esteem it can become very natural to think that the assigning and transferring of individual ownership rights is the very model and paradigm of practical thinking. Dealing with well-defined individual, subjective rights has great economic, administrative, and juridical simplicity. When these considerations of efficiency combine with views derived from residual religious beliefs, such as the belief in the infinite significance of each human soul, the idea that the world comes in neat packets of individual rights can even eventually infect our way of thinking about morality. It can come about that the only way people can imagine resisting economic and political oppression is by fictitiously creating a set of purported 'natural human rights'. This development may then in turn lead us to try to give our legal system further stability, by imagining it as grounded in a system of pre-determined 'natural or human rights'. The whole process can become a kind of self-reinforcing spiral with each turn making the notion of 'natural rights' seem more and more intuitively unavoidable and substantial.

Demand for greater administrative simplicity and efficiency are likely to be with us for a long time to come, and the peculiar combination of economic and legal systems which we see in advanced societies seems irresistibly set to encompass all parts of our social world more and more firmly. As a result of this we can expect ethics and politics to continue to *seem* increasingly to be transformed into a game in which a set of assigned imaginary counters, each representing some subjective right, is shifted around a board in certain at least partially predictable patterns. It will be increasingly difficult to avoid succumbing to this illusion and to resist the appeal of rights-discourse.

The second reason is that a doctrine of 'individual human rights' is connected in a plausible way with deep human needs and powerful human motives. These include the need for reliable control over objects of immediate use: 'it is *my* toothbrush and I wish to be sure that it will be in its place when needed; I have a right to use it as I wish and prevent others from taking or using it'. There is a strong element of wishful thinking involved here: if I insist on seeing the social world as a collection of rights, perhaps it will be true that what I take to be 'my rights' will be respected. The more powerless and isolated people feel, the stronger their attraction to a doctrine that assigns them an imaginary sphere of unrestricted and certain competence. There is, of course, also a fantasy which is in a sense the opposite of this one, and that is the nightmare of a 'closed' world run by administrators, bureaucrats, and lawyers.[52] I call this a fantasy that runs 'in the opposite direction' to the first because it seems obvious to me that the greater emphasis we put on rights, the more need we have of bureaucrats and lawyers – the experts in rights-discourse – to manage our world and lives for us. So far the second of these constructs has proved to have a less powerful hold on the popular imagination except in very limited contexts. Oddly enough, in popular political discussions one occasionally finds a strange amalgam of these two scenarios which overlooks their incompatibility, as if each of us could insist on his or her rights, but without the mediation of lawyers.

In some limited areas in a peaceful, well-functioning modern society, such as in conveyancing, assigning individual legal rights is a perfectly reasonable way to proceed, but the attempt to see politics *in general* through the lense of rights is one of the great illusions of our epoch. 'Rights discourse' is particularly well suited to play a central ideological role in current political theory. In addition to the two advantages mentioned above, it has the further ideologically advantageous property of being elusively polymorphous, and of allowing great variation in the detailed way in which any particular theory is elaborated. Virtually every theorist has his or her own variant which is distinctive in some way or other. This means that the general approach centred on the concept of a 'right' is difficult to get a cognitive purchase on; who has the time or energy to master all the variants? The general approach can always slip away and escape principled criticism in the disorder produced by its eager parturition of further monsters. The particular *pars pro toto* mistake on which rights-discourse rests is thus likely to be one that will haunt us for the foreseeable future despite our best efforts to be on our guard against it.

---

[52] Cf. Weber's fears about the modern world as a *stahlhartes Gehäuse (Gesammelte Aufsätze zur Religionssoziologie*, Tübingen: Mohr, 1920, vol. I, pp. 203f.) and Horkheimer and Adorno, *Dialektik der Aufklärung* (Frankfurt/M: Fischer, 1969).

Conclusion

A particular world-view dominates the contemporary political scene. It is composed of the assumption that societies should be organised as modern states conjoined with a commitment to a form of liberalism, democracy as a form of government, and a system of individual human rights. This conjunction, in my view, does not make much sense.

I have now discussed the state as a structure of coercion that is effectively unavoidable in the modern world and can never be fully voluntary, in any interesting sense of that term. It will always outrun what liberalism construes as its *de jure* legitimacy (in the philosophical sense). The coercive nature of the state is, thus, a basic obstacle to any completely harmonious cohabitation with liberalism, at least as long as liberalism remains committed to a principle of voluntariness. To the extent to which liberals have not simply tried to evade this issue, their attempts to deal with it have generally been sophisms; the polysemousness of the term 'freedom', however, makes these hard to detect.

Similarly, liberalism was born the sworn enemy of serious forms of democracy, and it is difficult to see how it can overcome this trait. The logic of the generation of a '*we*' of action is central to all forms of democracy; liberal individualism replies: 'You (plural), perhaps, but not me.' Radical democracy can abolish the state as a separate institutional structure, but it would be pretty clearly grossly incompatible with liberalism; indirect democracy cannot tame the state effectively. In the contemporary world liberalism is dependent on the state to enforce various of its favoured values (e.g. toleration, voluntariness), but it needs at the same time to try to limit state power. The barriers which liberalism can erect against the power of the state may seem substantial enough in times of peace and prosperity, but in times of serious political conflict they cannot be expected to hold. Tolerance, consensus, and voluntariness may work to ensure social peace and foster other positive values, if people want them to, but not everyone is committed to the principle of consensus, and it is by no means obvious that it is always rational for all agents to want tolerance and the principle of voluntariness to work. On the classic Marxist construction, it is not rational for those who are impoverished and oppressed to *want* universal tolerance and consensus-based reform rather than violent revolutionary change. Marx's economic analysis may have signal defects and he may have incorrectly identified the major class of oppressed people as 'the international proletariat', but his account of the specious logic of resistance to oppression retains its plausibility. Those who live in wealthy societies with a framework of robust institutions and strong liberal traditions can spend their time discussing the parish-pump politics that take place *within* that framework and the fine-tuning of the system of individual rights, but the framework is not in place everywhere in the world, and there is no reason to believe it will become universal in the foreseeable future. Even if one had no aspiration beyond that of extending the liberal system into new areas of the world, that would seem to require an ability to take a step back from it and see it in a slightly larger theoretical and empirical context. Such a wider context would be one in which the concept of a 'right' was to play a very derivative and subordinate role.

   Rights-discourse is a way of trying to immobilise society, to freeze it in an idealised version of its present form; not, of course, in its present *real* form, given that even recognised rights are rarely ever fully implemented in any society at any time. It is an attempt to ensure that the ghostly hand of the present is able to throttle the future. Whatever else they are, rights are fixed points and so can have no significant place in a society that has the flexible openness which Dewey, for example, valued in his version of democracy. A right, for Dewey, is the political analogue of the Kantian a priori in science. As we have been forced, Dewey thinks, to give up the a priori framework of Euclidean space for more flexible arrangements, so similarly a mature society will give up the doctrine of immutable individual rights. Such a doctrine can be made to sit comfortably with liberal individualism in some of its incarnations and perhaps also with the liberal desire to limit state power (although again one must ask who exactly is going to enforce these rights if not the state), but it is less clear that it is compatible with the principles of toleration and voluntariness. If no one has a right to interfere with me, do I have a right not to be tolerant? For that matter, what if I have uniquely great capacities for focused intolerance? Does the principle of individualism encourage me to cultivate them?

Similarly, although some rights are powers to do things, in all the versions of a theory of rights known to me, and in particular in any version that would be of interest to a liberal, some of the rights must be barriers to free action. Some barriers can be overcome with sufficient force or sufficient expense. Rights do not, then, utterly prevent voluntary transactions, but they do skew the landscape within which they operate to impose differential costs on agents seeking to act freely.

So is the conclusion to be drawn from this that the kind of liberal pluralism which is associated with Isaiah Berlin finally wins out? Berlin quite correctly noted that the main line of philosophy since Plato had tended to hold that the good was unitary in the sense that it was in principle possible for a state of affairs to exist which was maximally good in all respects.[1] Thus the society described in Plato's *Republic* is to be maximally self-restrained; also maximally just, wise, manly, and so on. It is, however, a commonsensical observation that in many realms of human life, although not in all, there exist values which cannot be co-maximised. To have an exuberant, vital, and spontaneous personality may be a good thing. To have a reflective, sober, and self-controlled personality may also be a good thing. It may be impossible for the same person to have both in the highest degree; realistically one might have to choose which to try to cultivate. Berlin claims that with regard to at least a wide variety of positive human properties and ideals – strength and sensitivity, equity and mercy, passion and asceticism – it is impossible to imagine a co-instantiation at the highest level, and the choice between them is in some sense a choice between incommensurables. The tension between conflicting demands is not something which could in general be abolished.[2]

There are, however, two distinct versions of pluralism, one liberal and one rather more existentialist. The liberal version states that there is a plurality of different goods among which one must choose without there being any single clear criterion for judging one good to be uniquely best. The tacit image of the world presupposed by the liberal version is of a place full of goodies with plenty for everyone: let all enter into the banquet of life and take their pick. There are limits to how much any one person can eat, and so eating some things carries a cost, the cost of not being able to eat other things that might in principle be equally tasty. The

---

[1] Berlin, *Four Essays on Liberty*.

[2] Weber at the turn of the century held similar views about the incompatibility of certain basic human goods, but was closer to what I have called the 'existentialist' variant than to the liberal one.

existentialist version is less sanguine: it is not just the case that one must choose, but choosing one good carries with it a cost that goes beyond the mere opportunity cost of missing out on other goods; this cost may, and usually will, include inflicting pain or visiting evil on oneself, or on others. The existentialist table is a small one; the crowd around it large. The good things on display are on the one hand generally pleasant and enticing, but each one of them contains a specific substance that nourishes some parts of the body, but also weakens and deforms others; furthermore, each dish chosen is not simply enjoyed instead of some other one, but potentially taken from the mouths of other people who might themselves be starving.[3]

The conceptual framework of contemporary politics which I have outlined is a highly complex abstract object, and some parts of it may well have the property that they are associated with values that cannot be maximally co-instantiated, so that an approach like that of Berlin is appropriate to them. However, *some* parts of this object, such as the doctrine of human rights, are, in my view, inherently confused, and some not only stand in tension with other parts, but are incompatible with them. This is a much bleaker view, I think, than that held by most liberal pluralists.

One might, nevertheless, be dubious about my whole theoretical approach. There is a family of very powerful lines of argument, instances of which have been developed by Burke,[4] Oakeshott,[5] Popper,[6] and Rorty,[7] which is predicated on significant scepticism about the possibility or desirability of 'abstract theorising' about politics, and Bernard Williams has offered arguments about the way in which reflection can undermine moral knowledge that could be thought to point in a similar direction.[8] I will examine three of these arguments.

First, it could reasonably be argued that politics is about action, and is a matter of tacit skills, practical insight, and the mobilisation of the imagination in the pursuit of collective ends, so that if one tries to reconstruct it as a matter of acting on general theories, one misses something crucial.

---

[3] See Colin Turnbull, *The Mountain People* (New York: Simon & Schuster, 1972).

[4] E. Burke, *Reflections on the Revolution in France.* (London: Dent, 1910).

[5] M. Oakeshott, *Rationalism in Politics* (London: Methuen, 1962).

[6] K. Popper, *The Poverty of Historicism* (London: Routledge, 1957) and *The Open Society and its Enemies* (Princeton: Princeton University Press, 1971) (2 vols.).

[7] R. Rorty, 'Postmodern Bourgeois Liberalism', in *Journal of Philosophy* (October 1983), pp. 583–9, 'Solidarity or Objectivity', in *Post-Analytic Philosophy*, ed. T. Rajchman and C. West (New York: Columbia University Press, 1985), and 'The Priority of Democracy to Philosophy', in *The Virginia Statute of Religious Freedom*, ed. M. D. Peterson and R. C. Vaughan (Cambridge: Cambridge University Press, 1988).

[8] B. Williams, *Ethics and the Limits of Philosophy* (London: Fontana, 1985), chapter 9.

A fortiori, then, it is claimed, one ought not to act on general theories in politics: they will not have high predictive accuracy, even if they happen to be accurate in a particular range of cases, they will not provide proper understanding, and using them will have a tendency to undermine the tacit skills that really are essential. One could also claim that terms which occur in political discussions do not have sharp edges, are not well defined, and are not even intended to be well defined, but they may be none the worse for all that. In practice, political 'theories' may refer to directions in which people are trying to focus interest and attention. Democrats urge the virtues of popular power, *étatistes* the need for state power, liberals defend the inviolability of individuals' lives, etc. Political 'theories', that is, are historically congealed kinds of rhetorical appeal which make use of certain quasi-propositional fragments. To hold such a theory does not amount to, and is not properly understood as, the assertion of a set of sober propositions that are intended to be taken as literal truths. One ought not in any case, it might further be argued, to fetishise consistency, and particularly in view of the above remarks about the nature of politics, it might be inappropriate to spend too much time and energy trying to point out purely theoretical problems: lack of clarity, ambiguity, purported contradictions. The relation between two areas both competing for limited resources of time and interest should not be seen as a relation of contradiction, especially given that in modern politics what counts as available resources will itself often be something that must be treated with a certain amount of flexibility. So there is not in principle anything wrong with saying that we need *both* a competent, efficient state *and* significant popular power. This might be thought to lead back to liberal pluralism.

The second line of argument might appeal to the thought that 'ideology' is at an end, by which is meant either the empirical claim that people are in fact no longer willing to act on large-scale, relatively speculative political theories, or that, although acting on small-scale and piece-meal theories is unobjectionable, acting on global ideologies is inherently dangerous and should be avoided (or both). However, not even the staunchest of the original devotees of the 'end of ideology' thesis thought that it was to be interpreted as precluding any significant role for general theorising in politics.

The third line of argument is a version of pragmatism which I will associate with Rorty.[9] Rorty seems sometimes to suggest that the end of ideological politics should mean the end of general theorising. To be

---

[9] See note 8 above.

more exact, he seems to conflate three things: (a) the end of ideology,
(b) Dewey's pragmatist criticism of traditional metaphysical and epistemological interpretations of the status of general theories, and (c) the end
of general theories in politics. Dewey held that serious thought is relative
to a concrete problematic situation. If the situation is not problematic,
enquiry is otiose. Much of traditional philosophy, he thought, consisted
in the generation of pseudo-questions which arose because of an inadequate appreciation of the way in which terms, concepts, and theories
were related to the concrete situations in which they originated.[10] Belief
was to be analysed by its reference to possible action directed at resolving
a problematic situation. If that is the case, one could argue, then to reject
all attempts at global, revolutionary reconstruction of society ('ideology')
means to reject all general political theorising as pointless and empty.
Pragmatists, however, have not generally held the extremely implausible
view that we would be better off without general theories altogether;
they have thought that we would be better off without certain pointless
philosophical discussions about the nature of theories, particularly about
the ontologies they purportedly presuppose.

There are, I think, two possible parallel mistakes that can be made
here: one is the complex of mistakes made by traditional philosophy
which arose from taking theories in too absolute and detached a way, and
resulted in the creation of all the conundrums of old-style epistemology
and metaphysics. The other, which is perhaps less dangerous because
less tempting, is to think that humans can be as the traditional Christian
God was conceived (by some) as being, and live entirely without discursive
concepts and general theories: that is, it consists in thinking that general
theories are more dispensable than they really are. If one liked that
way of talking, one could say that to think one could get away without
theories is to fall prey to a version of the metaphysics of presence. In
emphasising his opposition to those who make the first mistake, Rorty
occasionally seems to make the second. Just as, according to Dewey,
you cannot know a priori that space will be Euclidean or how property
should be distributed after a social upheaval, so you also cannot know

---

[10] Cf. Dewey, *Logic*. There is a way in which Dewey could be seen to converge with Nietzsche on the
one hand and Wittgenstein on the other. The later Wittgenstein thought that much traditional
philosophy consisted of attempts to scratch where it does not itch, i.e. where the situation is not
'problematic'. Nietzsche: If you are strong enough, certain things that are problematic for weaker
people will not be problematic for you, and so certain issues and questions will not even arise.
If one were ideally strong, one would not need theories. On some traditional theological views
God, the strongest being there is, has direct intuition and so does not need to use concepts or
theories at all.

antecedently at what level of generality an appropriate solution to a problematic situation will be found. In a world in which there is more contact between members of societies which are very different from each other than there has ever been before, the problems that arise are likely to be ones that can be resolved only if we have at our disposal theories of a rather high level of generality.

I see no reason to abandon the view that general theorising is an unavoidable part of what it is to be human, and thus that it is unrealistic to think we could get rid of it even if we had good reason to. This applies as much to politics as to natural science. The practically significant choice which we face is not whether or not to have a general view, but whether to have a more sophisticated, reflective, and more empirically informed view rather than a less reflective and informed general view. Obviously there is a loose fit between our general theories (which are controlled constructs of the human imagination) and the demands of action. From the fact that the fit is loose, though, it does not follow that there is no connection, and that there is literally nothing we could learn from a general theoretical study of politics which would improve our political practice.

The coherence and consistency with which I have been concerned here are obviously not identical to the formal consistency that was the goal of the Platonic search for definitions, although these virtues are also not completely unconnected with formal consistency in all cases. The analysis of such formal consistency is clearly an extremely blunt instrument that is of very limited use in the domains at issue here. After all, the Romans had what is in some sense a grossly contradictory set of views about slaves, viewing them in some contexts and for some purposes as people and in others as mere objects. This did not prevent the Roman Republic (and then Empire) from maintaining itself in a flourishing state for many centuries. Similarly Christians believed for millennia that God was both one and in three persons, that God was transcendentally differ-ent from man, but that Jesus was both God and man, etc. Even if purely formal consistency may be of limited value, the practical coherence of a set of political beliefs may be extremely important. The demands of this kind of consistency for a human political agent are not sharply defined – how could they be? – but this need not mean they do not exist. Politics is finally about acting, and action imposes some demands on us; in this context local forms of formal consistency may be highly impor-tant. Political concepts must be responsive to identifiable features of the existing political and natural world, must exhibit some conformity with whatever are the canons of plausibility and must retain connection with existing effective sources of human motivation. Of course, the pragmatist is right: philosophically sensible discussion of concepts and assumptions is discussion relative to a concrete envisaged context of use, and so a judgement of 'the coherence' of a set of concepts and assumptions is itself an evaluation made relative to a context, but modern political life provides the context (or, contexts) we need and there is no reason a priori to believe that it will not give us more than ample material for making such a judgement, one way or the other.

In this book I have focused my attention mainly on discussing, in a somewhat abstract way, some concepts that people have used and some doctrines that they have held. I think this is a valuable exercise. It would be highly desirable to have, in addition, an account which located these conceptions firmly in the world of the contemporary practical agent, connecting them with issues of motivation, subjective perception, real power, and valuation. If action is the goal we must know not only what is plausibly true, but also what will actually move people to act. Second, since the world of politics is a historical world, one would ideally want this practical account to contain a strong historical component, that is, to be 'genealogical' in the sense I take that term to have for Nietzsche and Foucault.[11] A final desideratum is that a full satisfactory account should be adequately *ideologiekritisch*, that is, that it should attempt to relate various political conceptions to the way in which human individuals and social groups see, and are perhaps deluded about, their interests.[12] I see these three further tasks as complementary to this investigation.

One can grant that the practical political agent is generally something of a *bricoleur*,[13] using the means that are to hand, conceptual and practical, modifying them for the purposes at hand, occasionally (very occasionally, perhaps) trying to construct something new, perhaps very occasionally stepping back to ask more general questions. We have, however, cre-ated some niches in our society (including such things as universities, academies, research institutes) precisely to allow some people to stand back from the pressing concerns of immediate political practice and ask how the toolbox can be improved. As Dewey was very keenly aware, the creation of such niches and institutions means a change in the kind

---

[11] Cf. 'Nietzsche and Genealogy', in *Morality, Culture, and History* (Cambridge: Cambridge University Press, 1999).

[12] I think, that is, that despite some remarks by Foucault apparently to the contrary, genealogy is compatible with some versions of *Ideologiekritik*. I cannot, however, pursue this any further here.

[13] C. Lévi-Strauss, *La pensée sauvage* (Paris: PUF, 1962).

of problematic situation we encounter. We now have not just pressing practical problems, but also theoretical problems. 'In the stage of development marked by the emergence of science, deliberate institution of problems becomes an objective of inquiry.'[14] As long as the people who devote themselves to theoretical problems, be they problems in physics or politics, remain aware of the ultimately practical nature of the undertaking in which they are engaged, their reflective labour is unobjectionable even to the most devoted pragmatist.

The contemporary political *bricoleur* is not trying to unblock the drains, but is engaged in actions that will affect, sometimes fatally, the life chances of many persons, and the 'tools' in the toolbox are now overwhelmingly concepts, words, images, theories, or fragments of theories. These concepts have histories; the theories generally claim to be internally consistent, and either rationally compelling or empirically well based. It is unlikely that one will be able to use them to any effect without having some general reflective grasp on some of their basic properties, just as it is unlikely that the *bricoleur* will have much success without practical acquaintance with the reliable empirical properties of the tools in the box.

The context of action sometimes imposes on us a deadly 'either/or', because as the final result of any given decision some may die while others will live (and perhaps even thrive). In addition much political action is directly or indirectly coercive. Kantian concerns with the non-contradiction of the will independently of any practical context are misplaced, but that does not mean that we can easily live with action-guiding theories that direct us to do incompatible things. Weber recognised that politics was in the final analysis about force, and that this meant that its appropriate everyday ethos was one of responsible reflection on the consequences of proposed actions.[15] Reflection on the consistency of political beliefs can be seen as an extension of this project. One can accept this as a contingent fact about our situation, and yet fail to find Kantianism at all plausible.

Unfortunately, we do not always know what the outcome of action will be – *who* exactly will live and who die. It is an unavoidable fact of the human condition that we sometimes must act on whatever is the evidence available to us, even though we know that that evidence is not conclusive. Some of the beliefs which I now hold and on which I base important decisions will turn out after the fact to have been false, but I don't know

[14] Dewey, *Logic*, p. 35.
[15] 'Politik als Beruf', pp. 549–60.

which ones they are. If, however, someone were now to demonstrate to me conclusively that some particular belief I hold is incorrect, I would think I ought to give it up. I would not think that this demonstration was irrelevant on the grounds that I already knew that some of my belief would turn out to be false. Similarly it may turn out that in retrospect historical agents are always conceptually confused, but that is no reason to embrace visible incoherence.

Bibliography

Adorno, T., Dahrendorf, R., Pilot, H. *et al. Der Positivismusstreit in der deutschen Soziologie.* Neuwied and Berlin: Luchterhand, 1969

Allen, D. *The World of Prometheus: The Politics of Punishing in Democratic Athens.* Princeton: Princeton University Press, 2000

Assman, J. *Moses the Egyptian.* Cambridge, Mass.: Harvard University Press, 1998

Baier, A. *Moral Prejudices.* Cambridge, Mass.: Harvard University Press, 1994

Ball, T. *Transforming Political Discourse.* Oxford: Oxford University Press, 1988

Barry, B. 'Is it better to be powerful or lucky?', in *Democracy and Power.* Oxford: Oxford University Press, 1991

Berlin, I. *Four Essays on Liberty.* Oxford: Oxford University Press, 1969

Berman, M. *All that is Solid Melts into Air.* New York: Simon & Schuster, 1982

Bittner, R. *Moralisches Gebot oder Autonomie.* Freiburg and Munich: Alber, 1983

Bloch, M. *Feudal Society.* Chicago: University of Chicago Press, 1961 (2 vols.)

Burke, E. *Reflections on the Revolution in France.* London: Dent, 1910

Cohen, G. A. *Karl Marx's Theory of History: A Defence.* Oxford: Oxford University Press, 1978

Constant, B. *De la liberté chez les modernes: Ecrits politiques,* ed. M. Gauchet. Paris: Hachette, 1980

Dewey, J. *The Influence of Darwinism on Philosophy.* New York: Holt, 1910
  Logic: The Theory of Inquiry. New York: Holt, Reinhardt, and Winston, 1938
  The Public and its Problems. New York: Holt, 1927
  The Quest for Certainty. New York: Minton, Balch, & Co., 1929

Dewey, J. and Trotsky, L. *Their Morals and Ours.* New York: Pathfinder Press, 1973

Dostoyesky, F. *Notes from Underground,* trans. C Garnett. New York: Dell, 1960

Dumont, L. *Homo hierarchicus: The Caste System and its Implications.* Chicago: University of Chicago Press, 1970

Dunn, J. *The History of Political Theory and Other Essays.* Cambridge: Cambridge University Press, 1996
  Interpreting Political Responsibility. Princeton: Princeton University Press, 1990
  Western Political Theory in the Face of the Future. Cambridge: Cambridge University Press, 1993 (2nd edn)

164   *Bibliography*

Dunn, J. (ed.). *Democracy: The Unfinished Journey*. Oxford: Oxford University Press, 1992

Durkheim, E. *La division du travail social*. Paris: PUF, 1986
'L'individualisme et les intellectuels', in *Revue bleue* 10 (1898)

Elster, J. *Sour Grapes: Studies in the Subversion of Rationality*. Cambridge: Cambridge University Press, 1983
Ulysses and the Sirens: Studies in Rationality and Irrationality. Cambridge: Cambridge University Press, 1979

Farrar, C. *The Origins of Democratic Thinking*. Cambridge: Cambridge University Press, 1988

Finer, S. E. *The History of Government*. Oxford: Oxford University Press, 1997 (3 vols.)

Forrest, W. G. *A History of Sparta*. New York: Norton, 1968

Foucault, M. *L'histoire de la sexualité: La volonté de savoir*. Paris: Seuil, 1976
'Le nuage et la poussière', in *L'impossible prison*. Paris: Seuil, 1980
Power/Knowledge, ed. C. Gordon. London: Harvester, 1976
Surveiller et punir. Paris: Gallimard, 1975

Frankfurt, H. G. 'Freedom of the Will and the Concept of a Person', in *The Importance of What We Care About*. Cambridge: Cambridge University Press, 1988

Gadamer, G. *Die Vernunft im Zeitalter der Wissenschaft*. Frankfurt/M: Suhrkamp, 1980
Wahrheit und Methode. Tübingen: Mohr, 1960 (2nd edn)

Geuss, R. 'Auffassungen der Freiheit', in *Zeitschrift für philosophische Forschung* (1995), pp. 1–14
'Freedom as an Ideal', in *Proceedings of the Aristotelian Society*, Supplementary Volume LXIX (1995), pp. 87–100
'Der Freiheitsbegriff im Liberalismus und bei Marx', in *Ethische und politische Freiheit*, ed. J. Nida-Rümelin and W. Vossenkuhl. Berlin: de Gruyter, 1997
The Idea of a Critical Theory. Cambridge: Cambridge University Press, 1981
Morality, Culture, and History. Cambridge: Cambridge University Press, 1999

Habermas, J. *Moralbewußtsein und kommunikatives Handeln*. Frankfurt/M: Suhrkamp, 1983
'Wahrheitstheorien', in *Wirklichkeit und Reflexion: Festschrift für Walter Schulz*. Pfullingen: Neske, 1973

Hampshire, S. *Justice is Conflict*. London: Duckworth, 1999

Hansen, M. *The Athenian Democracy in the Age of Demosthenes*. Oxford: Blackwell, 1991

Hare, R. 'The Lawful Government', in *Philosophy, Politics, and Society: Third Series*, ed. P. Laslett and W. G. Runciman. Oxford: Blackwell, 1967

Hayek, Fr. *The Constitution of Liberty*. Chicago: The University of Chicago Press, 1960

Hegel, G. W. F. *Grundlinien der Philosophie des Rechts*, in *Werke in zwanzig Bänden*, ed. E. Moldenhauer and K. M. Michel. Frankfurt/M: Suhrkamp, 1970 (originally 1821)

Bibliography

Heidegger, M. *Holzwege*. Frankfurt/M: Klostermann, 1950

Heine, H. 'Zur Geschichte der Religion und Philosophie in Deutschland', in *Beiträge zur deutschen Ideologie*, ed. Meyer. Frankfurt/M: Ullstein, 1971

Hirschmann, A. *Exit, Voice, and Loyalty*. Cambridge, Mass.: Harvard University Press, 1970

The Passions and the Interests. Princeton: Princeton University Press, 1977

Hobbes, T. *Leviathan*, ed. R. Tuck. Cambridge: Cambridge University Press, 1996 (2nd edn) (originally 1651)

Hohfeld, W. *Fundamental Legal Concepts as Applied to Judicial Reasoning*. New Haven: Yale University Press, 1923

Hollis, M. and Smith, S. *Explaining and Understanding International Relations*. Oxford: Oxford University Press, 1990

Horkheimer, M. *The Eclipse of Reason*. New York: Oxford University Press, 1947

Horkheimer, M. and Adorno, T. *Dialektik der Aufklärung*. Frankfurt/M: Fischer Verlag, 1969

Humboldt, W. von. *Ideen zu einem Versuch die Grenzen der Wirksamkeit des Staats zu bestimmen*. Stuttgart: Reclam, 1967 (originally 1795)

Kant, I. *Kritik der reinen Vernunft*, ed. R. Schmidt. Hamburg: Meiner, 1956

Zum ewigen Frieden in *Kant Werkausgabe*, ed. W. Weischedel. Frankfurt/M: Suhrkamp, 1977, vol. XI

Kierkegaard, S. *Concluding Unscientific Postscript to the Philosophical Fragments*, Princeton: Princeton University Press, 1992 (originally 1846)

Kropotkin, P. '*Anarchism*', in *The Conquest of Bread and Other Writings*, ed. M. Shatz. Cambridge: Cambridge University Press, 1996

Lacan, J. 'Kant avec Sade', in *Ecrits*. Paris: Seuil, 1966

Lévi-Strauss, C. *La pensée sauvage*. Paris: PUF, 1962

Lukacs, G. *Geschichte und Klassenbewußtsein*. Neuwied and Berlin: Luchterhand, 1968 (originally 1923)

Lukes, S. *Individualism*. Oxford: Blackwell, 1973

Power: A Radical View. London: Macmillan, 1974

Manin, B. *Principles of Representative Government*. Cambridge: Cambridge University Press, 1997

Margalit, A. *The Decent Society*. Cambridge, Mass.: Harvard University Press, 1996

Marx, K. *Grundrisse der Kritik der politischen Ökonomie*. Berlin: Dietz, 1953

Marx-Engels Werke. Berlin: Dietz. Verlag, 1957ff.

Mill, J. S. 'On Liberty', in *'On Liberty' and Other Writings*, ed. S. Collini. Cambridge: Cambridge University Press, 1989 (originally 1859)

Mills, C. W. *The Power-Elite*. New York: Oxford University Press, 1956

Montaigne, M. *Essais*, ed. M. Rat. Paris: Garnier, 1962

Morgenthau, H. *Politics Among Nations*. New York: Knopf, 1948

Nietzsche, F. W. *Die fröhliche Wissenschaft* in *Kritische Gesamt-Ausgabe*, ed. G. Colli and M. Montinari. Berlin: de Gruyter, 1967ff. (Vol. III) (originally 1882)

Jenseits von Gut und Böse in *Kritische Gesamt-Ausgabe*, ed. G. Colli and M. Montinari. Berlin: de Gruyter, 1967ff. (Vol. v) (originally 1886)

Zur Genealogie der Moral, in *Kritische Gesamt-Ausgabe*, ed. G. Colli and M. Montinari. Berlin: de Gruyter, 1967ff. (Vol. v) (originally 1887)

Nozick, R. *Anarchy, State, and Utopia*. New York. Basic Books, 1974

Oakeshott, M. *Rationalism in Politics*. London: Methuen, 1962

Olson, M. *The Logic of Collective Action: Public Goods and the Theory of Groups*. Cambridge, Mass.: Harvard University Press, 1965

Peters, R. 'Authority', in *Political Philosophy*, ed. A. Quinton. Oxford: Oxford University Press, 1967

Plato. *Republic*, ed. G. Ferrari. Cambridge: Cambridge University Press, 2000

Plato. *Opera*, ed. J. Burnett. Oxford: Oxford University Press, 1902

Popper, K. *The Open Society and its Enemies*. London: Routledge, 1971

The Poverty of Historicism. London: Routledge, 1957

Rawls, J. *A Theory of Justice*. Cambridge, Mass.: Harvard University Press, 1971

Raz, J. *The Morality of Freedom*. Oxford: Oxford University Press, 1986

Rickert, H. *Die Grenzen der naturwissenschaftlichen Begriffsbildung*. Tübingen: Mohr, 1921 (4th edn)

Rorty, R. *Contingency, Irony, and Solidarity*. Cambridge: Cambridge University Press, 1989

'Postmodern Bourgeois Liberalism', in *Journal of Philosophy* (October 1983), pp. 583–9

'The Priority of Democracy to Philosophy', in *The Virginia Statute of Religious Freedom*, ed. M. D. Peterson and R. C. Vaughan. Cambridge: Cambridge University Press, 1988

'Solidarity or Objectivity', in *Post-Analytic Philosophy*, ed. J. Rajchman and C. West. New York: Columbia University Press, 1985

Rousseau, J-J. *Du contrat social*. Paris: Garnier, 1962

Émile ou de l'éducation. Paris: Garnier, 1964

Russell, B. *Power: A New Social Analysis*. London: Allen & Unwin, 1938

Ryan, A. *John Dewey and the High Tide of American Liberalism*. London: Norton, 1991

Schumpeter, J. *Capitalism, Socialism, and Democracy*. London: Allen & Unwin, 1943

Shklar, J. *Ordinary Vices*. Cambridge, Mass.: Harvard University Press, 1984

Simmons, J. *Moral Principles and Political Obligations*. Princeton: Princeton University Press, 1979

Skinner, Q. *Liberty Before Liberalism*. Cambridge: Cambridge University Press, 1998

'The state', in *Political Innovation and Conceptual Change*, ed. T. Ball, J. Farr, and R. L. Hanson (eds.). Cambridge: Cambridge University Press, 1989

Taylor, C. 'What's Wrong with Negative Liberty?', in *The Idea of Freedom*, ed. Alan Ryan. Oxford: Oxford University Press, 1979

Taylor, Michael *Community, Anarchy, and Liberty*. Cambridge: Cambridge University Press, 1982

Tocqueville, A. de. 'De la démocratie en Amérique', in *Oeuvres, papiers, et correspondances*, ed. Méyer. Paris: Gallimard, 1951
Tuck, R. *Natural Rights Theories: Their Origin and Development*. Cambridge: Cambridge University Press, 1979
'Why is Authority such a Problem?', in *Philosophy, Politics, and Society*, ed. P. Laslett, W. G. Runciman, and Q. Skinner. Fourth series. Oxford: Blackwell, 1972
Tucker, R. (ed.) *The Marx–Engels Reader*. London: Norton, 1978
Turnbull, C. *The Forest People*. New York: Simon & Schuster, 1972
The Mountain People. New York: Simon & Schuster, 1972
Waldron, J. *Liberal Rights*. Cambridge: Cambridge University Press, 1993
(ed.) *Nonsense upon Stilts: Bentham, Burke, and Marx on the Rights of Man*. London: Methuen, 1987
(ed.) *Theories of Rights*. Oxford: Oxford University Press, 1984
Weber, Max *Gesammelte Aufsätze zur Religionssoziologie*. Tübingen: Mohr, 1900.
Gesammelte Aufsätze zur Wissenschaftslehre. Tübingen: Mohr, 1973
Gesammelte politische Schriften. Tübingen: Mohr, 1980
Wirtschaft und Gesellschaft. Tübingen: Mohr, 1956
Westbrook, R. *John Dewey and American Democracy*. Ithaca: Cornell University Press, 1991
Williams, B. *Ethics and the Limits of Philosophy*. London: Fontana, 1985
Winch, P. 'Authority', in *Political Philosophy*, ed. A. Quinton. Oxford: Oxford University Press, 1967
Wolff, R. P. *In Defense of Anarchism*. New York: Harper & Row, 1998 [1970]
The Poverty of Liberalism. Boston: Beacon Press, 1968

Index

CPSIA information can be obtained
at www.ICGtesting.com
Printed in the USA
LVHW010422291119
638734LV00008B/696/P

9 780521